More Books From the Author:

111 Tips to Create Impressive Videos
How to Plan, Create, Upload and Market Videos

111 Tips To Make Money With Writing
The Art of Making a Living Full-time Writing –
An Essential Guide for More Income as Freelancer

111 Tips on How to Market Your Book for Free:
Detailed Plans and Smart Strategies for Your Book's Success

111 Tips to Get Free Book Reviews:
Best Strategies for Getting Lots of Great Reviews
1,200+ reviewer contact links

111 Tips to Create Your Book Trailer
How to Create, Where to Upload and How to Market Your Video

Book Marketing on a Shoestring

How Authors Can Promote their Books
Without Spending a Lot of Money

© Copyright 2018 Doris-Maria Heilmann

Publisher: 111Publishing

All rights reserved under International and Pan-American Copyright Conventions. No part of this book may be reproduced in any form or by any electronic or mechanical means, including information storage and retrieval systems, without permission in writing from the author.

Print Book Edition ISBN: 978-1-988664-22-4
Electronic Book Edition ISBN: 978-1-988664-21-7

111 Publishing, 21 Crockett Ct, Antigonish, NS, Canada

Introduction *1*

PART ONE

Why Book Marketing is Important – and Rewarding 5
How Readers Will Find Your Book 8
Author-Entrepreneur – Do You Have What it Takes? 9
Marketing Possibilities Seem to Be Overwhelming 10
The Internet is Full of Bogus Stories 11
What's the Difference Between Marketing and Selling? 11

PART TWO

Evaluate Your Current Publishing Situation 15
Let's Start With the Basic Tasks 17
Professional Author Portrait 18
Your Avatar 20
Join the Most Effective Social Media Sites 20
Use Your E-mail Signature 27
Join Reader/Writer Communities – Online and in Person 28
Start a Website and/or a Blog 30
Sell Your Books from Your Website/Blog 37
Create a Business Card and Bookmarks 37
Outline an "Elevator" Pitch 39
Start a Newsletter E-mail List 40
Write Blog Articles as a "Guest Blogger" 42
Write Prequels for Your Future Novel 44
Contribute Content to Article Directories 44

PART THREE

You Never Get a Second Chance for a Good First Impression 47
Write a Compelling Blurb 50
Keywords are Important! 51
Edit, Edit, and Edit Even More! 53

Increase Readership: Create an Audiobook ... 56
A Print Version of Your Book – Will it Sell More Copies? ... 58
Get an ISBN Number and Register Your Copyright ... 60
Why do you Need a Copyright Registration? ... 61
List Your Book Worldwide ... 61
Create Excitement With a Book Cover Poll ... 62
Gather as Many Early Reviews as Possible ... 62
Advance Book Reviews ... 65
Get Pre-Orders For Your New Book ... 67
Pre-Orders on Apple iBooks ... 67
Get Pre-Orders on Your Website ... 68
How to Deal With the Media and Book Bloggers ... 69
Create a Media Kit ... 70
Submit Photos of Your Book Cover ... 71
Get Help From Journalists ... 73

PART FOUR

Find Marketing Steps Inside of Your Book ... 77
Choose the Right Book Category/Genre ... 83
Let Your Readers Pay With a Tweet ... 84
Press Releases for a Review – Are They Worth the Effort? ... 86
Create a Separate BOOK PAGE or AUTHOR PAGE ... 87
How to Organize Your Book Launch Party ... 91
There Are Dozens of Online Book Retailers ... 99
With a Little Help from Your Friends… ... 106
Get More Book Reviews ... 107
Cross Promotions and Blog Tours ... 108
Create a Slide Show for Your Book ... 109
The Power of Book Trailers ... 110

PART FIVE

Book Marketing Strategies ... 113
Selling Books and e-Books to Libraries ... 115
How to Get Your Print Books into Airport Bookstores ... 117
Offer Your Book to Book Discussion Clubs ... 119
How to Profit from an Award ... 120

Get Interviews on Radio and TV Shows.............................. 121
Improve Visibility for Your Books 122
Connect All Your Social Networking Sites 125
Book Signings at Local Bookstores 126
Get Your Book Translated Into World Languages 127
Sell Your Foreign Rights 129
How About a Movie Deal for Your Book? 129
How Else Can You Leverage Your Manuscript? 132
Bestseller Tips – From Trade Publishers 137
CHECKLIST FOR YOUR BOOK MARKETING 148

About the author *153*
Note to Readers *155*

Introduction

You may not be a New York Times bestselling author with a publicist – yet. If you want to succeed at self-publishing, you'll want to learn everything you can about professional book layout, publishing, and traditional book marketing methods.

During the last years roughly nine million new self-published books have appeared. Almost all are available on online retailers' websites. In addition, these titles will be offered for many years to come. Most of them are in digital format and will never go "out of print". The "gold rush" seems to be over, and author-publishers have to compete for readers with major publishing houses/media conglomerates, who jumped finally on the e-book bandwagon.

> IMPORTANT: You will find many steps during the publishing process when reading this book. These tasks are not obvious "book marketing" tasks, but they are essential for your success as an author. For example: having an appealing book cover, choosing the right genre, placing your book into the worldwide *Bowker* – *http://www.bowker.com* – listing, and writing prequels for your next books.

One trait for writers is essential: patience. So, don't be discouraged if it takes a while to build your author brand and improve your book's ranking. The more you write – not only books, but also magazine/newspaper articles, blog posts, guest blog articles, Google+ posts, and short stories – the more exposure and success you will have.

Writing is a joy and it is also part of your book marketing and platform. It typically takes FIVE books to start making a living from your work.

For Whom is this Book Useful?

- You might belong to the group of talented authors who have written a fantastic self-published first novel – but you just don't have the sales numbers your book deserves. You realized that selling and marketing is a completely different process than writing and publishing your book. You are not alone. Very few writers have a degree in marketing and business or experience in publishing and selling on- and offline.

- You may have crafted several thrillers, or non-fiction books, and found a publisher who accepted your manuscripts and published your first book (after two long years). Your book is then available in bookstores, but it isn't displayed on the best-seller tables at the store's entrance. You had to search for it in the shelves and found it finally – spine outwards – among lots of competing titles. In addition, the clock is ticking: you found out from your agent that bookstores return all unsold books after a couple of weeks to make space for the next "bestseller" shipment.

- Or you could be a writer who, after ten or twenty rejections from all the major publishers, and finally signed up with a "publishing" company (aka vanity publisher). You have already paid $2,000 to bring your book to the market. Unfortunately, you have to promote it yourself or pay this company another $5,000 for a press release and the "possibility" of a radio or TV interview. Because your financial resources are somewhat tight, you decide to market your book on your own – at least for now.

Dear Reader,

No Money? No Problem! Success in social media book marketing, using the tools described here, is almost all free. A certain time commitment may be necessary, at least in the beginning, depending on your level of involvement. Yet, the more you use these marketing tools, the faster you can handle them. This means that you will get more visitors and buyers.

This book's title promises "Marketing Your Book for Free". That's true for all your activities except for three that you will use to start your platform:

- Your professional Author Portrait
- Your Website/Blog Hosting
- Your Business Card/Bookmarks

These tools are a (small) necessary expense unless you are good friends with an excellent portrait photographer, website designer/host, or maybe even a print company. Otherwise expect to pay around $150-$200. However, peanuts when compared to starting a different business. That's what it is: a publishing business (if you want to sell your books). Or it is a hobby… writing just for the fun of it, not bothering with professional publishing.

PART ONE

Why Book Marketing is Important – and Rewarding

It doesn't matter if you plan to write as a hobby or to earn money. You may be only thinking about writing a book, and you have so far crafted merely the first outline. You will still benefit from learning the key marketing steps any author can take to create a platform from which to promote their books. Many of these steps are small, some can be achieved in minutes!

Others take longer or must be implemented as regular tasks. Don't start with the goal to sell a lot of copies of your first novel; start with the goal to create a relationship with your future readers. At the same time, work on your next title. If readers like your first book, they won't want to wait two or more years until your next one comes out. They will want to see the sequel soon. Otherwise, they will find another author. Remember, they can choose from millions in each genre.

Publishing your books is one thing, but getting those books to the readers who buy and read them is another. Ideal fans and readers are gained one by one at a time, and it takes months to build a bond, even if you experience suddenly a lot of exposure. The first step is to find out:

- who these readers are
- what they like
- what they're willing to pay for your books

- where they hang out
- how they like to communicate

There are easy and free ways to find this information. You're probably not going to be surprised, but the first place you should head is your nearest Google search bar. Google knows more than anyone about what's going on online. It's up to us to learn how to use this fantastic resource to find our readers. Let's say you write about glider flying. Use Google to search form "glider flying forums" and "aviation discussion boards." If your hero in a novel is a tennis aficionado, use "tennis forums" and "tennis discussion boards."

You are going to get a lot of hits to research, and you will find some very active communities with engaged people talking about your specific topic. Some of these forums are quite large, and you might need to drill down a bit to find the sections that apply to your specific niche, but this will put you in immediate contact with people interested in your topic.

- Another great way to find your readers is through blogs in your niche. Blogs that have been online for a while will have a readership of some size. Do a little research to find the blogs that have the most readers interested in your topic. For instance, if you found a discussion forum, check the links that belong to frequent contributors there, and you will start to connect to the blogs in your niche. Look at the comments on popular posts and start exploring the comment links for even more places where readers are hanging out. Usually, the link is embedded in the name of the person or their avatar.

Become an Active Member of Reader Forums

There are more reader forums and communities than Goodreads or LibraryThing, and commenting, reviewing other writer's books, and sharing their news and blogs will result in many friends and readers. On Goodreads and LibraryThing book lovers are actively looking for new reads. And besides Amazon, these are the next best places to get book reviews.

The e-book market numbers exploded as big publishers went into digital formatting just as independent authors do. Now, major publishers use their backlist inventory to transfer these manuscripts into e-book versions. This means that their bestseller and mid-list books won't go out of print anymore.

One after the other of the big trade publisher conglomerates have started selling their books via Amazon. This new trend makes it even more important than it was five or ten years ago to have a large following of loyal readers. As they would say in real estate: "It's a buyer's market, not a seller's market!" Self-publishing guru, Aaron Shepherd, sums it up: "The party is over".

So, you have written the best book and found the best agent possible. And you made the best deal with the best publisher. In that case, you will be surprised to learn about the reality of traditional publishing: publishers do spend little money on advertising, PR and paid placement in bookstores. But, they don't spend the same amount on all books. In fact, they spend almost all their marketing budget on bestselling authors. On average, publishers shell out less than $2,000 on advertising 90% of their titles (mostly only for listings or ads in their bookstore catalogs). That's not much exposure to get the word out about your book.

It all adds up to this fact: no matter how you publish or plan to publish, it is up to YOU, the author, to market your book(s). The more you learn about professional book promotion, the easier it will work for you. You will also have more success. In this one and several upcoming guides to publishing and book marketing, you will learn in detail how to achieve it!

How Readers Will Find Your Book

A Pew Survey shows how people find books, in this order:

1. Searching on Top 100 Bestseller lists
2. Shopping for books written by their favorite author
3. Trustworthy Media Recommendations
4. Word of mouth, or word of mouse
5. Book search by genre or keywords
6. Meeting the author in person (or online)
7. Deals, discounts or free book campaigns

New writers might not be able to tap into #1 bestseller lists, but they can foster relationships with their readers. This will help to establish a loyal following of many readers who buy, read, review and recommend their books. A loyal group of supporters will also help to promote #2, #4 and #6 books by their favorite author through word of mouth and in person or online promotion. However, as an author, you still need to know where and how to find your target readers as well as how to plan your professional marketing strategies.

Author-Entrepreneur – Do You Have What it Takes?

Even as a "shy" writer you will be able to learn the basics of book promotion. Don't be intimidated. Remember: One can eat a whole elephant or whale. They just need to be split up into small, plate-size portions. The same is true of every long-term goal. What's important is that you spend at least half an hour a day on your author platform, your brand, and networking with your future readers. Make it a habit to work at a certain time on your "book business". Don't wait until a huge amount of tasks build up.

Make a plan. You will find sample checklists and marketing suggestions at the end of this book. Structure your day and stick to your plan. The earlier in the writing process you start working on your book promotion, the more progress and success you will achieve.

Difference Between Platform and Brand:

What "platform" and "brand" means for writers: An author platform is the position and tools from where you create your brand. Your brand is what defines you. It's the way your readers recognize and see you. Your platform can be a website, a blog, or social media accounts. It can also refer to any of the following: an event, such as a book signing; or, places from which you operate and build your author brand.

Your brand is how readers and the public recognize you. You, as a writer, will build your own brand, in the same manner as Stephen King or James Patterson. They are brands. We know what to expect from their book covers and content. Apple is also a brand. It's not just a brand name. To the public, it invokes a certain image and perception. People know what to expect from the brand in terms of product, quality, design, and so forth.

Marketing Possibilities Seem to Be Overwhelming

Becoming an author-publisher is a long-term commitment and requires hundreds of small steps on the path to success! Few authors are actively planning their book and its promotion. They only think about getting help when frustration sets in. However, throwing lots of money into advertising is costly and might be only a rather short-term solution in the best-case scenario. Creating a long-term brand, and a platform from where you can communicate with your readers, is more efficient for the following reasons: it is almost cost-free, and it gives the author a solid base for the promotion of future books. A writer's best promotional tool is her writing. Advertising costs money. New articles and short stories make money. It doesn't matter if it's a book, magazine, or newspaper article. Magazine and other freelance writers are more successful when their stories are popular with readers and generate lots of comments. An important duty for writers is to build a platform and a brand to extend the readership. The same is true for professional bloggers, who often run several affiliate programs on their blogs.

For you as an author to get lots of traffic (and clicks) on

your blog and raise their Alexa and Google Search Engine rankings, you need to promote your writing. Short story markets will allow new readers to sample your work – readers you would never reach otherwise. Sampling really works! Have fun writing. If you have fun, you readers will have fun, too.

The Internet is Full of Bogus Stories

Don't be discouraged by writers who claim to have sold hundreds of thousands of their books in a short time or claim bestseller status in order to cash in on these stories. (I bought some of these "success-stories" years ago, but will never, ever buy a book from them again or recommend those writers). When you look behind the scenes, they have either paid for hundreds of reviews (such as John Locke) or a service company bought tens of thousands of their own books (which these authors had to advance). These are two of the methods by which authors can catapult themselves to the New York Times *Bestseller status* – http://savvybookwriters.wordpress.com/2013/03/04/the-dark-sit. All of this false hype causes writers to think their book is a failure if it is not showing up on bestseller lists. Wrong!

What's the Difference Between Marketing and Selling?

There are two avenues: the marketing and promoting part and the selling of your work. It doesn't matter if you self-publish, or if you have sold the rights for your manuscript to a traditional publisher. Either choice presents two options:

- **Invest money** to buy ads, go on book signing tours, attend book fairs, and sell to bookstores
- **Invest time** to build a platform and create an author brand through the use of social marketing and most of all: content marketing, such as articles and short stories.

We can also split it into:

- the promotional, social part
- the "hard-selling" part

The hard-selling part will barely work if you have not laid the foundation. Would you be likely to buy something from an unknown person online or offline? Remember that your competition in published books is fierce. There are millions of new books published every year. Since the large trade publishers have also gone into the e-book business and will transform their complete book backlists over time into e-books, the competition will rise even more. This is what it means for you as an author: you have to compete with well-known, professionally-created titles and established authors who are already a household name. Why would readers buy an unfamiliar book from a totally unknown author?

Marketing strategies will, in essence, be the same for both fiction and non-fiction: The foundation for your book's success is in building a community, a social environment, and a platform from where you can introduce yourself and your work to readers. How can you accomplish this even before your book is finished, better yet, even before you start writing? I will show you in Part Two!

It takes at least a year to make oneself known in the reader community. Start early in order to have a successful book launch. Other benefits of joining and participating include: gaining knowledge, avoiding costly errors, and sometimes even receiving ideas for your own writing process or book content.

Writing is a creative, often solitary work. Writers do need to market their books by connecting and networking with potential readers. That's the only way they'll sell their books. However, there is a difference between promotion and sales. The promotion and marketing of your book is the ongoing drive to keep your book in the public eye by whatever means. On the other hand, the selling of your book involves direct requests to buy it. Aggressive (hard) selling is a real turn off for your audience, as it is in any industry.

The process of networking (meeting your future readers online or in person) should be fun for both sides. The interaction should not consist solely of continual "Buy my book!" requests. If your readers like you and your writing, they will buy it anyway. This is especially true if they have had a chance to "sample" your work.

Make sure that your readers can sample your work through blog posts, magazine/newspaper articles, and social media posts. In this case, you are not selling anything directly. You are giving people a taste of your work – for free. This generates buzz. People will talk about you on social media, and they will link to your site from their blog.

PART TWO

In this chapter we give you, in chronological order, the basics to start your author platform. Later, you will find even more details in the sequel to this book:

111 Tips on How to Market Your Book for Free.
https://www.amazon.com/dp/B018RA72LY/

Remember: The construction of a house always starts with the foundation, not with the windows or the roof. Your writing and publishing career is the same! You start with your platform and grow from there. It involves many details, including the following: publishing or distributing quality writing online through the medium of blogs, newsletters, websites, or articles in magazines and newspapers, and taking part in social networks to meet your target audience. Don't give up – it all takes time!

Evaluate Your Current Publishing Situation

- Are you giving readers what you have to offer, or are you giving readers what they want? Ask yourself the following questions, and mark each one where improvement is needed:

- How large is the market for your book in numbers? Did you thoroughly study your competition? Who, exactly, will be your audience? Is it a popular genre, or more of a niche? Is your book in the right genre? Did you choose the full potential of categories at online retailers, which can be boom or bust for your book?

- What is your publishing situation? Traditional publishing? Author publishing? Vanity publishing, or contracting with an aggregator? Do you own your ISBN? Do you have access to your online retailer's publishing account? What is the duration of your publishing contract? Does it contain a non-competing clause?

- What was your previous marketing strategy? What worked and what didn't? Did you have a book launch, re-launch, or any special promotions? How often and how well was your book reviewed? In which promotion did your publisher invest? Is it positioned properly?

- What is your following on, and involvement with, social media? Do you have at least 1,000 Goodreads friends, 2,000 Twitter followers, and the same numbers on Google+? Have you joined reader communities on Google+, Goodreads, Wattpad, LinkedIn, LibraryThing, KindleBoards, etc? These might be numbers only, but did you choose the right keywords? Pick some from your book's content and genre. In addition, in order to find quality followers, use keywords such as "avid reader", "reading", "book lovers", "book reviewers", "book blogger", "book club", "love to read", "amreading" and "bookworms".

- Did you create additional separate author/book pages on Twitter, Goodreads, Google+, Pinterest, Facebook, LibraryThing and other communities?

Does your author page at online retailers need improvement?

- Do you show off your writing skills? Are you regularly writing blog posts? Does your website have a prominent button on your sales pages? Do you write guest blogs on influential book bloggers' pages?

- What are your activities related to getting book reviews? Have you sent out press releases in order to get interviews, radio or TV appearances or features in magazines/newspapers? Are you following book bloggers and reviewers online and in person? Do you write positive comments on their blogs?

- How do you approach reviewers? Have you joined reader/writer communities on Goodreads, or made friends with their most popular book reviewers?

- What are your long-term goals? Where will you be as a writer in one to three years? What will be your author brand, and how will you be different from other authors in your genre?

Let's Start With the Basic Tasks

These are tasks that can be accomplished long before you write your book, or somewhere in between the writing of your first word and the publication of your book. Don't wait until your book is already for sale. Start early preparing yourself for success!

You Never Get a Second Chance for a First Good Impression!

Every writer, no matter if she or he is trade-published, self-published, or freelance, needs to show professionalism in her/his appearance. A great author portrait for books, websites, and magazine or reader community page avatars is equally important. Study the bestsellers in your genre. Learn how their publishers present these authors and their books. Follow their websites and blogs. Wonderful opportunities to learn!

Professional Author Portrait

Do you want to be seen as an amateur? For sure not! Professional authors have photos taken by portrait photographers. This is immensely important for any author – no matter what genre you write. You can't use a Facebook photo, not even a high-quality wedding image that you might have cropped to show only your head. In addition, you shouldn't use a snapshot that is unflattering and uninteresting, has a cluttered background, or has an out-of-focus image.

No party or holiday photos including several people or your partner, nor images including your dog, or your toddler. This is what tops them all: some authors show an image of their car, dog, or cat, instead of a portrait or headshot. I cringe every time I see these images because not only are your readers and customers on social media sites. Literary agents and publishers, as well as journalists, are too.

Professional Author Portrait

Every author needs a professional portrait. If you promote yourself and your book, you will need one! A photo can do wonders in terms of giving you credibility and establishing trust. Prices for these photos vary greatly, depending on the location, the experience, and popularity of the photographer. The honorary can vary from less than $50 to approximately $500.

An author photo is an important piece of your brand. If you have a professional photo that you like, you can use it for years. You can use it everywhere: on your books, in articles, for promotional material, or for your social media avatar. When people see it, they will think of you and your writing. Have a look at the famous photos of people like J.K. Rowling and Stephen King. Discover how they convey so much at a glance. Choose your photographer by looking at the photographer's website. If possible, meet him or her before you make your decision.

Order your portrait in several sizes to use it for a variety of illustrations, not only for your author page or your book cover, but also for social media and your blog. Not everyone is an expert in Photoshop or other image enhancing programs.

A book's back cover will often include the author's photo. On a hardcover, the photo and biography are mainly placed on the back flap. The book's back cover is used for blurbs and reviewer comments. Typically, paperbacks have the sales copy, an author photo, and a brief bio on the back cover. Get both: a black and white glossy print and a full-color cover. Certainly, get both in digital format: jpeg and TIFF (for print). This way you can use the images for decades and for many purposes.

Make sure the photo reflects your personality. Have your expression match your personality. For instance, if you are considered a pretty upbeat person and you are usually smiling, a pout would look unnatural. The author photo needs to give the viewer a good sense of the persona of the author. Most of all, you should be close up enough so that your face fills almost the whole format. It should also be a well-composed and effective photograph of high-resolution quality. In this over-exposed world of cyberspace, your photo may stay with you for a very long time. Ask yourself how you want to be seen by the world.

Your Avatar

Your avatar and your description on social media sites are your introduction to future readers. What do you want them to know about you? Writing a bio is one of the hardest things to do. Allow some time while you are in this stage to find some important keywords that define you and your books. If you come up with some great new phrases, update your other social media biographies; your message should be consistent across social channels. Just copy and paste your "master bio" and use the same bio and avatar on all public appearances. Don't forget to include a link to your website or your Amazon author page!

Join the Most Effective Social Media Sites

I must add that they should be the most effective sites for authors, in particular. If you are relatively new to social media, always remember: it is not a selling tool, but rather a *networking* place – *http://savvybookwriters.wordpress.*

com/2014/05/27/a-myth-selling-books-through-social-media: It might take many months to get a hold there, depending on your interactions. So, don't expect a flood of followers and book readers shortly after you have joined. The first 1,000–2,000 followers are the hardest to find; but, once you gain traction, followers will flock to your site. To explain every social media site, one could write several books. (maybe I should write them.) However, I have already written many blog posts about how to navigate Google+, Twitter, Goodreads, and LinkedIn. Why did I choose these four sites?

Google+ (or GooglePlus)

Everything you post here goes directly to Google's search engines if you click the public button before you hit "send". You can post up to 500 words, which is almost a whole blog post. Don't forget to add a great image to each post and a link to your blog or author page. You can place your book's cover and a description of your novel at least once a day in your Google+ stream once you have enough followers there. Don't forget that you can post all your events, such as book signings and book launches, on Google+. It is free! You can even add a map that shows how to get there.

Connect Google+ with Twitter and you save lots of posting time. The fantastic SEO (Search Engine Optimization) effect cannot be stressed enough! If you want people to find you or your books, make Google+ your number one social media site. Did I mention that you can open several accounts? You can open one for each of your books and start up to 50 Google+ reader communities if you want.

Google+ communities are for users who are more interested in vibrant conversations about topics rather than about self-promotion. Quality community members are those who share relevant content that sparks conversation or debate as well as participate in conversations by leaving comments and +1'ing posts. Posts within a community are indexed by Google and will be found in organic search results. This means you will have a higher ranking on Google's search engine!

Start your own Google+ Community. When you own or moderate a Google+ community, you can create categories to organize discussions, remove offensive content, and highlight great posts. You can also add moderators to help you keep the conversation going, invite members, or edit your community. Invite up to 500 people to join your community at a time. You may increase the number of posts in your community and encourage others to use it as you add more members. Here's a tip: anyone can share a community by clicking the "share this community" button. When you click it, you'll create a Google+ post that links to the community's page.

Twitter

Here are some tips for this site: follow others, tweet something valuable for others, and don't use Twitter only as a cheap way to advertise! Create a nice mixture of your own: interesting tweets blended with re-tweeting. If you want to become popular on Twitter and have your tweets go viral, learn how to use Twitter in a smart and social way. Also, nurse your relationships. They are the reason for Twitter's existence. Find out what to avoid on

Twitter in one of our blog posts – *https://savvybookwriters. wordpress.com/2014/04/21/17-social-media-mistakes-to-avoid-on-twitter-2*.

Goodreads

Start early on this site and add up to 25 book enthusiasts per day until you hit several thousand. Open a second page for your books on Goodreads and connect your blog with your Goodreads profile. They have a great feature in their help section: a slide show on how to navigate Goodreads. A month before your print book's launch, start a giveaway (for e-book giveaways use better LibraryThing) of one, three or maybe even five books. If you are lucky, hundreds will apply, which means you will know exactly who is interested in your book. Goodreads lists them on your Giveaway page. "Friend" these people right away! There are not only readers and writers on Goodreads, but lots of bloggers and book reviewers. In addition, there are thousands of communities for every genre and topic you can imagine. More on *Goodreads* in a blog post – *https://savvybookwriters. wordpress.com/2013/10/15/7-top-reasons-for-writers-to-be-on-goodreads/*.

LinkedIn

LinkedIn is a social network with now over 500 million users. But LinkedIn is much more than a social site. It's a community of professionals and it is THE place, particularly if you are a writer or publisher. Almost 95 percent of all editors and journalists are on LinkedIn, which makes it easy for writers to connect with them.

Join any or all of the best groups for writers on LinkedIn. Read also the descriptions of the best 20 groups for writers. You will make fulfilling connections if you choose the right followers and carefully create an appealing (search-engine-optimized) bio. Join any or all of the *best groups for writers – https://www.leelofland.com/the-20-essential-linkedin-groups-for-aspiring-writers/* – on LinkedIn. Read the descriptions of the best 20 groups for writers.

Here's a great way to find new readers for your books: blogging on LinkedIn. Use this new, free feature to get more exposure for your writing and your books. The Twitter function helps to have all your LinkedIn posts automatically pinged to Twitter. If you use custom graphics or images, you have the additional benefit of adding a visual element to your profile as your three most recent posts on LinkedIn are part of your profile. Your connections are notified each time you publish a post on LinkedIn. You are also encouraged to send a note to your own Twitter and Facebook followers. Posting long-form content on LinkedIn should be a priority in your marketing efforts.

More Tips for Social Media Networking:

- Create an attractive profile using the professional portrait from your avatar, you can even use the same description. Choose your own background image, not the generic one.

- In order to save time for interactions with your followers, get the help of (free) post scheduling software, such as Hootsuite.com or Futuretweets.com. Set them up in a way to post at the same time on several sites, such as Google+, Twitter, and Facebook.

- Again: choose your following carefully. You want to interact mainly with readers, book bloggers, and reviewers – not only other writers. The question is: How do you find readers? All social media sites have a search function at the top of the page. Useful keywords to type in include the following: book bloggers, read, reading, book lovers, book club, love reading, bookworm, love to read, mystery book reader, science fiction reader, avid readers, readers, word nerd, non-fiction book blogger, reading books, reviewing book, and even librarian. Click on "people" or scroll down a lot, since the first names that appear are often publishers and other commercial accounts.

- You can also type in the names of successful books in your genre and find readers there, talking about those books. Follow those readers who you feel belong to your book genre based on what they say in their tweets. Re-tweet their posts, engage in meaningful conversation, be funny, or refer to blog posts you wrote; but, don't mention your book. They will find out about it soon enough. It's a subtle way to build your network and promote your book.

- Be professional. Set-up your bio with a studio portrait, the same one you use in your books. Create an inviting avatar. Use key words that will attract the type of people with whom you want to connect. This bio (or avatar, or "about me") can be used for all your profiles, for your Amazon website, your blog, and so forth. The same holds true for your photograph.

- Once your bio is established, you can use it everywhere. You may have to shorten it for some sites, such as Twitter. Use lots of keywords and add abbreviated links to your website or Amazon page. Also, choose your username wisely!

- Understand the meaning of social media: being SOCIAL and NOT constantly talking about your book! I noticed a writer on Twitter who tweets 100% only about his book. He seems to use automatic tweets, as he never, ever engages in any conversation with others. For sure, I was not the only one who un-followed him.

Here are a few other suggestions to get you started:
- Write about interesting things that are happening
- Give valuable advice
- Engage in a humorous way with your readers or post inspirational quotes?

Follow these basic rules for your online platform: find the right followers (readers), be "social", and have a professional appearance. These are the keys to successfully promoting your books. For more social media networking tips check out this *article* – *http://savvybookwriters.wordpress.com/2013/11/17/which-social-network-is-best-for-authors*.

Conclusion: Social Media is Not for Hard Selling!

It is what the name says: a social place. You wouldn't go to a party because you want to sell your books there. You go to a party to meet people, socialize, and have fun. Not all the social media places are equally well situated to help members meet new people who may become future readers.

Networks like Facebook and LinkedIn often restrict their connections and information to people with whom you are already acquainted. Choosing someone new on LinkedIn often requires that you confirm their email address. On Facebook, you are punished if you choose too many followers with whom you weren't previously connected. More about the differences in social media can be found in a *Bloomberg Businessweek article – http://www.businessweek.com/articles/2013-03-08/facebook-vs-dot-twitter-want-your-feed-filtered-or-unfiltered*.

Use Your E-mail Signature

Never send out an email without your author signature. You have probably heard this advice before: you can use e-mail signatures to market and promote your books.

Every day you send out e-mails to friends, business colleagues, your lawyer or accountant, and potential clients and readers. If you have an e-mail signature, you are constantly sending people "passive" marketing. You are spreading the word about you, your brand and your books. It's pretty easy: click on your e-mail's "tool" or "settings" function. Create your e-mail signature right now!

Join Reader/Writer Communities – Online and in Person

Achieve your book-marketing goals through online activities in a fun way: most writers already like to hang out in cyberspace, networking, and blogging. Once you have created an avatar – this includes your author portrait, a short bio, and a link to your blog/website – you can follow book bloggers in your genre and comment positively on their articles or book reviews. Each time you do so, you leave behind a link to yourself, your website, or your blog. If people who read your comment find what you have written interesting, they will click on the link to find out more about you. Then, they may decide to become regular blog readers or subscribers, newsletter subscribers, or book buyers.

Join forums (other than reader forums) that are associated with the keywords in your novel or non-fiction book. For example, if you write a novel that takes place in historic places, then join a group of historians and learn more about the time and place where your story is located. Aside from the benefit of your book's research, you will meet people who are already interested in the topic.

If you drop a hint about your writing, they might eventually become readers, even fans, of your work. Here's an example: let's assume you are writing a romance and the heroine is invited to travel with her lover to Argentina to meet him at his family home. Wouldn't it be great to meet people from this country and get first-hand information about places and customs? You could even pick up some Spanish idioms!

- Even in the early stages of your career, try to connect with influential people who you can later ask to read and review your book(s). Do the same with reader communities, such as Goodreads, Wattpad, Shelfari, LibraryThing, etc. As an author, it is a MUST to be a member of these communities and a free (other than your time) way to introduce your book(s) and show your book titles.

Join also Scribd, RedRoom, BookTalk, KindleBoards, Booksie, or Bibliophil. Post snippets (or chapters) of your book to excite potential readers on Wattpad. Throughout their careers, many writers are posting their stories on this highly popular site. Even established, traditionally published bestseller authors such as Margaret Atwood, as well as aspiring writers who are just expressing themselves, are using Wattpad. Learn more about these and many more *reader communities – http://savvybookwriters.wordpress.com/2012/03/11/18-top-websites-to-promote-your-book-for-free*.

IMPORTANT: Join reader communities for the purpose of social networking, not book advertising. People can read your avatar as well as find your website, or Amazon URL, there. There's no need to mention your work ten times a day, or reference it in every comment you post.

Meet Readers and Writers Groups

I am sure you have heard about *Meet-up Groups – http://www.meet-up.com/*: People all over the world meet in their city with folks who have the same interests. You can join for free and attend casual meetings of freelance writers and journalists as well as beta-reader and writing critique groups. This is a fantastic way to exchange tips, get writing reviews, and learn from others. There are more groups besides Meet-ups.

Just ask your local libraries (where meetings often take place), or google your keywords and your city or town. These groups are all fantastic networking opportunities too. Are you a member of a book-reading club? There are often dozens of groups in cities. Why not join one to learn more about reading critiques, possibly meet book reviewers, and (in the future) maybe offer your own books for discussions? There is no better pastime than for writers to meet book lovers!

Start a Website and/or a Blog

A blog is one of the most valuable tools to show you and your work to readers. You certainly can incorporate your blog into your website. This article explains how to create a *mobile-friendly website* – *http://savvybookwriters.wordpress.com/2014/08/29/5-tips-how-to-create-mobile-friendly-blogs-and-websites*. Another one explains the key to a *successful author website* – *http://savvybookwriters.wordpress.com/2014/04/07/the-key-to-a-successful-author-website*.

Once you have press clippings and articles about your book published, scan them and add them to your website. While a website is static, a blog is better suited to boost your search engine rankings. Every time you write a new post, you get a new URL "in the eyes of the search engines". Your blog is part of your platform and your author brand. Your blog has endless benefits, such as:

- higher "Search Engine Ranking" on Google,
- better visibility for you as a writer
- constant contact with your present and future readers
- lots of material for posts and tweets

Other benefits of a blog include the following:

- You can leverage it as a portfolio
- If you have enough articles, you can convert it into a book
- Readers can sign-up for your newsletter
- It will separate you from mainstream writers

Many traditional websites only have five or six pages. The maximum number of times they will ever get indexed by search engines is five or six, if they are static (not constantly updated) pages. However, when you create a blog, every single post you publish has its own URL. Suddenly you can go from five or six pages to twenty, fifty, a hundred or more.

> **IMPORTANT: Install "Follow" buttons on all your social media sites. And add "Share" buttons to your website/blog, so that readers can send and recommend your blog posts or websites all over the Internet.**

Blog reader surveys found that blogs are building trust and influencing buying decisions. Blogs serve as the best tool for increased online visibility because they are constantly updated. This makes them attractive to search engines. The more visible you, your book, your website, and your blog become, the more traffic (readers) your blog will attract. This signifies that you are finding more buyers for your book now, or when it is released. To create a successful blog, write often and consistently on the subject of something about which you feel passionate. That's all it takes.

Blog Regularly

Static websites don't attract many new clients or customers. However, a regularly updated blog can produce a constant stream of new readers from all around the world. Blogs have so much influence on purchase decisions. When readers sign up, they expect to be able to read new content from you at least once or (even better) twice a week.

What Shall I Blog About?

Start with what you have already written: tiny snippets of your book as well as research you found in the pre-writing stage. You can also re-write, or spin, a short chapter of your book. For example, you can explain more to your readers about the place, the time, the weather, landscape, or history and anything else related to specific scenes from your novel. You can even write about restaurants that the protagonist patronizes. Please see our blog post on *FREE, Brilliant Book Marketing – http://savvybookwriters.wordpress.com/2013/07/07/free-brilliant-book-marketing-to-a-million-audience*.

Create Web or Blog Content Without Writing

You have no time to write? No problem! There are so many ways to create content for your blog:

- Photos
- Videos
- Podcasts
- Re-blogging
- Slide-Shares
- Guest posts
- Infographics
- Lists
- Snippets from your book
- Polls / Surveys
- Research pieces from your books
- Curating other blog articles

Your Blog is Your Inventory

Use it! When it comes to updating your blog, the more frequently you do so the better. Set a schedule for blogging, for instance, every Monday and Thursday. Read other related blogs as well as comments on posts, forums, or books to get ideas. In addition, write down your own experiences in writing or publishing—including the answers you found when looking for solutions. Use your own photos to illustrate your blog or magazine articles, or upload free photos from a variety of *photo sites – http://savvybookwriters.wordpress.com/2013/05/06/where-can-you-find-free-photos-and-illustrations*.

How to Promote Your Blog

The best way to spread the word about your blog is blog directories. Here just a few:

http://blogs.botw.org/Arts/Literature/Publishing/

http://www.bloggeries.com/Writing_Publishing/

http://technorati.com/company/about-us/

Learn to Write for the Web

Web visitors don't read – they scan text. Learn how to write for the web: lots of bullets, headlines, sub-headings, and images. Also, use the "inverted pyramid", starting with a summary and then go from most important to less. Write interesting page titles that grab attention, structure your text, and write summaries at the end of each chapter. Readers spend more time on pages with valuable information, structured and easy-to-read content. You will also want to add lots of links for better SEO (search engine optimization), which will boost your Google ranking.

Submit Your Blog to Social Media:

Google+, Twitter, Pinterest, Tumblr, and LinkedIn. Be on at least Google+ and one more of these networking sites. Click on "public" and "extended circles" when posting on Google+, and your content will be immediately picked up by Google's search engines! Therefore, Google+ is the most important social media site for writers!

If you share interesting links (and your blog posts), and offer great free information, you will quickly become a favorite in these social networks. Your followers and connections on social media will later become your fan base. They will read and subscribe to your blog posts and newsletters. Eventually, they will buy, read, recommend, and review your books.

> IMPORTANT: As soon as you have a presence on Goodreads and LinkedIn, and an author page on Amazon, connect your blog with these sites. All articles will show up there within hours and improve your readership numbers tremendously. It leads to more exposure for you and your writing.

There is so much you can do to let your articles and blogs, or website content, go viral on the Internet. It takes a little bit of effort, but the results in a couple of months will be rewarding. Also, the longer and more often you post, the easier it gets. As Robert Kiyosaki (author of *Rich Dad, Poor Dad*) said: "The richest people in the world build networks. Everyone else looks for work." Write content and reach out. The creation of an author platform belongs to the same project as the book you write. Leverage your creativity. Just a reminder: write lots of content, such as: guest posts, blogs, and short stories for weblogs, websites, magazines or newspapers.

The Benefits of Owning a Website

If you own a website or blog, you will get all the search engine rankings that you wouldn't get with "free" websites (such as Weebly, WordPress.com or Wix) where you are

NOT the owner of the site. You can add your own plug-ins, opt-in email address form for future newsletters, follow-me buttons, affiliate programs, etc. All this is not possible if you choose a "free" website. Depending on the contract, the site owners might even own the copyright of your content and images. They place their own advertisement on the site; you would deliver "free content" for them. Please consider: what happens when these companies fold one day?

All your articles and images will be gone. This is one more reason why it just looks tacky to have a Weebly website. If you run a professional website (an author blog, a publishing business, a portfolio), then you are much more likely to need total control over everything, from hosting to advertising, branding, sales, and more.

Before you or your web designer start creating your website or blog, make a *plan – http://savvybookwriters. wordpress.com/2014/01/23/5-tips-for-a-perfect-author-website* – that should cover at least these points:

- Easy to Read
- Easy to Navigate the Website
- Easy-to-use Links to Other Sites
- Contact Form for Visitors
- Sales Page (e-Commerce for Your Books)

Read more about how you can get *lots of visitors and book lovers – http://savvybookwriters.wordpress.com/2013/05/16/ how-to-get-lots-of-visitors-to-your-author-website* – to your website.

Sell Your Books from Your Website/Blog

While you are creating your website, incorporate an ordering system for your reader to purchase the book directly from your site. Self-publishing authors can certainly sell books from their own website. There are several benefits:

- You will have higher revenues (almost 100% of your book's sales price)

- You will get paid faster (immediately when someone orders – not three or six months later)

- You will know your readers (which is rarely true when you sell through stores or online retailers)

This article explains how to set up an *online store – http://savvybookwriters.wordpress.com/2013/12/18/why-sell-your-books-from-your-own-website* – on your website in detail. Find more practical tips in *111 Tips on How to Market Your Book for Free – https://books2read.com/u/bMre1a.*

Create a Business Card and Bookmarks

Print business cards to advertise yourself as an author and add all the web addresses where your books can be found. Hand the cards out to everyone you meet and post the cards on community bulletin boards at bookstores. You should also add them to each book you ship out. Inexpensive print options can be found here:

- *http://www.digitalroom.com/secure/products.html*

- *http://print24.com/us-en/product/business-cards/*

- *http://www.veraprint.com/Default.aspx*
- *http://www.vistaprint.ca*
- *http://www.eprintfast.com/businesscards.html*

Consider these Options Before You Order Your Cards:

- Include a picture of your book(s) on one side. This is as important as including your name.

- Have a tagline that differentiates your book from others, especially others in the same genre.

- Include ways to reach you, such as your Twitter, Google+, Amazon, and blog/website links.

- Don't give out your phone number. As a writer, you need to control if, when, and how you are interrupted.

- Use your (your own) publisher's logo. Even if you've started your own publishing company, putting a logo on the card will give you some added credibility. (People won't know it's your own company)

Instead of handing out a business card, give this more casual, but attractive symbol to people such as book lovers, friends, family, colleagues, acquaintances, book club members, and visitors at fairs or conferences. It ought to show the cover or another image from your book's content. The card should be colorful and artistically designed, printed on both sides, and show the title of your book in bold letters on the bookmark's top or bottom. In addition, you certainly want the reader to visit your website or blog. Don't forget to add the URL as well as a link to your Amazon or D2D author page.

Get Price Quotes. Ask your business card printer for pricing; also, search the Internet for price and quality comparisons. Find some of the many companies who produce bookmarks in a *SavvyBookWriters blog article* – http://savvybookwriters.wordpress.com/2014/02/19/how-bookmarks-promote-your-books.

Outline an "Elevator" Pitch

This is the 30-60 second description of the benefit of reading and buying your book. It's called an "Elevator Pitch" because it describes the challenge: "How would you explain your book or your business if fate placed you in an elevator with your dream prospect. Imagine you only had the time it takes to get from the bottom of the building to the top to give them your pitch?"

The purpose of an elevator pitch is not to sell something. It's to interest the other person in continuing to talk or to hear more about it. It's a sort of "teaser". Your pitch should be 30 to maximum 60 seconds. It needs to end with a question, "call to action", or another appropriate closer, such as: "Does that sound like something you would look at, or that interests you?"

This allows the listener to respond. If they are interested, they will ask questions. Content is as important as your delivery. If the content of a pitch is uninspiring or uninteresting, it won't matter if it's well-delivered and the perfect length. There are differences between verbal and written pitches; between the way people speak and the way they write. If you are able to write dialogue as a writer, then you are also able to tell your elevator pitch to someone in a natural and conversational way.

Start a Newsletter E-mail List

Should you get in touch with your readers through e-mail? Why not? Would you like to let your readers know about your book launch, book cover reveals, new blog posts or book signing events--maybe even articles relating to your book's content? Newsletters via email offer more customized ways to contact your readers than social media.

Ask any serious blogger about the biggest blogging mistake they have made. All of them will tell you the same thing: their biggest regret is failing to set up an e-mail list as soon as they started their blog. I am guilty of this as well. I started two years too late!

Money is not an issue, nor is it difficult to set up a list. MailChimp.com is free if your email list is under 2,000 email subscribers. You can try out AWeber.com for just $1. Adding a sign-up form for your readers to the sidebar of your blog is simply a case of copying and pasting some HTML code.

How Do You Grow Your Newsletter Email List?

Nothing is easier:

- Ask your social media followers and friends via tweets/posts

Start A Newsletter E-mail List

- Add a sign-up form to all your blogs and websites
- Create an opt-in link in your e-book
- Invite readers at book signings to opt-in for your newsletter

E-mail newsletters drive 1350% more traffic than social media, and they outperform other marketing channels. Also, they help you stay connected with your readers, not only at times of a book launch.

Start a spreadsheet, or list, with names and e-mail addresses of everyone who signed up for your newsletter. Include the names of potential readers. Use it as a back-up. You never know what can happen with (Internet) companies. This way you have your own list of your readers/customers.

As a smart writer, you also have an external hard drive and/or memory sticks with the latest content of your computer; it should also contain everything else you have ever written. Store this data in a safe place outside of your home! Computers can implode; houses can burn down; and, thieves can take valuable items. No insurance company will ever pay for your lost manuscripts and years of work!

> IMPORTANT: The GDPR – rules of the European Union that regulates the privacy of online users – which applies to anyone who has an email newsletter, a blog, website, or sells over the internet. It's enough to have only ONE single user from Europe. If you have a place where people can sign up for your newsletter, you must also make sure that they can opt out of

the newsletter later. This is easiest done by adding an "Unsubscribe" link at the bottom of each email you send.

If you collect data at the point of sale, you must state how you store, use, share, and maintain security on your website with this data, including name, address, phone number, email, and payment details. Online portal SelfPublishingReview offers authors to download their "FREE Privacy Policy Template For Author Websites – GDPR". Download it here: *http://bit.ly/2vLLJNx*

Write Blog Articles as a "Guest Blogger"

Guest blogging is a great way for your blog and your book's sales page to get some fantastic exposure. You certainly can add links from your guest blog via the re-blog function to your website, your own blog, or the online retailer where your book is sold.

Be careful for whom you write. Check the blog's *Alexa Ranking – http://www.alexa.com/*. The lower the Alexa Rank is the better. Set a limit of 500,000 (out of almost a billion websites and blogs that are roaming cyberspace). Here are a couple more tips:

- Your Guest Post must be original. It should be a new, original post, written entirely by you
- Don't use articles from article directories
- The length of your guest blog should be approx. 500 to 800 words
- Exclusivity will usually be for 30 days

- Use examples and anecdotes to clarify your points
- Offer fresh content that has not been published before
- Ensure that your post does not violate any copyright laws
- Have a conclusion at the end of your article
- Have a call to action for readers after the conclusion

IMPORTANT: Learn to Write for the Web. Writing for blogs is totally different from writing a novel. Learn how to write in the "inverted pyramid" style: the most important information goes on top, the less important information goes further down in the text.

Is your text easy to read? Eye-tracking studies have shown that readers SCAN text (in an F-shaped pattern), rather than READ it. Also, website visitors read more slowly on the screen than in print. Very important: make yourself familiar with the statistics about headline success and which ones are the *most popular* – *http://savvybookwriters.wordpress.com/2014/08/22/5-tips-to-gain-readers-with-great-headlines*. A catchy blog headline is a reason people are reading it.

Writing guest blogs is a fantastic way to gain new readers. In addition, you are not limited to book blogs. Why not offer guest posts to *The Huffington Post, Salon.com* or *The Atlantic*? The most important step is to read these publications first (the content listings) and check to see if a similar topic was covered in the last year. If the topic was covered, see which angle it was written from, in order to avoid duplication. Follow submission guidelines to the letter.

Once you have a portfolio of blog articles, you might also offer blogs and essays to magazines that are paying well.

Write Prequels for Your Future Novel

Use your blog to write about your next book. You can write one, or several prequels. A prequel can be one story or a dozen stories, and even a short ebook. However, it should be an irresistible preview of the book itself. It should be short but include a revealing scene from the draft manuscript of the novel. It can be a great teaser for the upcoming work. The author's goal should be to make the reader want more. It is never too early to write a prequel. You might write it even before you begin to write your book. Your blog is a great place to do just that. However, keep it to a maximum of 1,500–2,000 words and don't reveal too much. It should be only a teaser for your next book.

Contribute Content to Article Directories

Recycle or rewrite parts of your blog posts or book manuscript into short articles you can post in content farms or e-zine article directories. Almost all of them have a resource box for a short bio and a link back to your website, book, blog, or subscription form. These articles are picked up by other bloggers, newsletter editors, e-zine editors, and so forth. Each time your resource box (short bio) is featured, readers click on your links to find out more about you, subscribe to your blog and newsletter, or purchase your book.

All these steps in PART TWO can be prepared before you write, or before you even finish your book. In fact, the more of these steps you climb – well in advance – the easier and more successful your book marketing activities will be. Remember, these tips are an overview only. More details can be found in the sequel to this book: *111 Tips on How to Market Your Book for Free* – https://books2read.com/u/bMre1a

PART THREE

In this chapter, I will show you important steps in your book's production. Let's assume your manuscript is finished, has been read by other writers and beta readers, and is on the way to the editor. What is your next step in book marketing? You will need to professionally prepare your manuscript for the book's launch.

You Never Get a Second Chance for a Good First Impression

A stunning book cover is one of the best marketing tools for any writer! E-books are bought online, usually displayed on a page with many other books. Use simple, yet stunning graphic elements and bold, clear text for the title and the author's name. Both must be easy to read on the tiny, stamp-size online image. Interesting book covers get more exposure on shelf displays, both online and off-line. We are a visual culture, which influences our book-buying habits too.

Check out all the books that are similar to yours. Place your book (or a mock-up) between these competing titles. Does it look better? Is the spine eye-catching? Ask other patrons what they think about every book, but don't tell them which one is yours. Listen to their opinion. Place your book on the first table in your favored bookstore, right where the New York Times bestsellers are piled. Does your book cover really stand out?

Check if there are specific, or popular, sizes in your book's genre. Do all these steps BEFORE your book is ready to print. Later changes will only confuse readers and cost you more money. Discuss these points with your cover designer:

- Use of bold or complementary colors
- Use light on dark for dramatic effects (if it fits your book content)
- Use no more than a total of two different fonts
- Don't use wide vertical spaces between lines of text
- Use shadow, bevel, gradient or glow effects sparingly; keep it subtle
- Align the cover text to center, left, or right
- Place text on a plain background to stand out
- Let the front cover design flow into the book's spine
- Use the same fonts for all your books; readers will be able to identify them easily
- Test the cover in thumbnail size to make sure it looks good on Amazon's website

More *tips for great book covers* can be found in a former blog article – *http://savvybookwriters.wordpress.com/2014/03/23/the-best-and-the-worst-book-covers*.

Your Brand is Your Signature

We distinguish between "Series Branding" and "Author Branding". Visual author's brand is also called "Author

Identity": You see a book cover without reading the text and you know it must be from this or that author.

Author branding is how you represent yourself to the entire industry and create a recognizable and trusted name. A brand is about how you want your audience to perceive you as a person and a professional. Strongly branded book covers can also have a huge, positive impact on your chance of gaining media attention or getting bookstores interested in stocking your books. Cover designer Aimee Coveney lists these essentials:

- a strong, unique font for your author name and book title
- similar illustrations or image styles for each book
- consistent layout
- maybe even the similar use of color

Multi-Piece Designs: It should be the same cover style and one element (the author's name for example) in the same font and font size. An example is the Chicken-Soup series of inspirational and motivational books.

Series Branding: Use either a signature element in different cover concepts or a one-design-concept and then change small elements.

Get 15 branding examples in this *"Adrijus" article* – *http://www.rockingbookcovers.com/book-cover-design/different-ways-to-brand-book-covers-for-series/* – including a useful book cover design checklist to learn what to think about, what to prepare and what to communicate with your cover designer.

Write a Compelling Blurb

Your book's cover design and a catchy title are of primary importance. A superb blurb, full of brilliant keywords, is the second most important sales pitch for your readers. Blurbs are not only sales pitches. They give the reader a comprehensive summary of what the book is about. Blurbs can also wet the buyer's appetite for reading or buying the book. It should excite the reader to buy your book. At the least, it should inspire the buyer to view the "Look Inside" section of an e-book, or open the paperback version and browse through the chapters.

Learning how to write a short blurb for your book can be fun. But it is also a helpful practice for writing promotional short articles of any kind – especially for online copy, which should always be short and concise. Blurbs cannot only be used for your book's back cover, they can also be incorporated into the following:

- proposals for publishers
- your e-book's online sales page on Amazon, Kobo, B&N, etc.
- your website page, or your blog's "About" page
- submissions for contests
- "Writer in Residency" applications

Other people also may have a use for your blurb:

- Editors and publishers will need it for an article on you and your book
- The person introducing you in an interview or a writers' panel will also need it

Tips on Writing a Book Blurb

- Blurbs can range from a few lines to a few short paragraphs. A book blurb does not provide answers, but rather spark the reader's curiosity.

- First, you must determine the market for your story

- Most of your success will depend on your opening line – the hook or the headline

- Write your blurb in a way that shows your potential reader how you will deliver

- End with a reason for the reader to buy/read your book. It can be in the form of a statement or a provocative question

- Study lots of back cover blurbs in your own, or a library's shelves

- If it's a novel, it should promise a fabulous, entertaining read. A non-fiction or self-help book blurb should promise a solution, or appeal to the reader's interest.

Whoever picks up the book (or finds it online) and reads the blurb should think, "I must read this book!" *More tips on writing blurbs – http://savvybookwriters.wordpress.com/2013/08/08/how-to-write-a-brilliant-blurb-for-your-book* – can be found in one of our blog articles.

Keywords are Important!

Ever wondered why similar books get different amounts of readers or book popularity? If topics and quality of the content are comparable, then the reason is almost always the "right keywords" – or their lack of…

To improve book sales at all your online retailers, you need to use the right keywords – which can be found easily on Amazon. It starts already with optimizing your title and subtitle, and certainly your book description, and product page blurbs. To achieve this, research on Amazon all and any books that are similar to yours. Why searching on Amazon? What works for Google keywords may not necessarily work on Amazon or other online book retailers!

Amazon belongs together with Google and YouTube to the world's largest search engines. No matter if Google or Amazon searches, they both respond better to keyword strings/keyword phrases as to single keywords. Find at least two or three words that you can string together before you add a comma. Amazon allows up to seven keyword strings, other online retailers often up to ten.

Keywords are not single words only. Ask yourself: what do you type into Amazon's search function when looking for a book in a certain genre or a certain topic, maybe a thriller, happening in the medical field? Do you type in: Novel? eBook? Thriller? Hospital? For sure not! At least you will type in "medical thriller" or better: "medical thriller doctor patient" or "medical thriller hospital 2018" or "medical thriller nurse hospital" – which are all suggestions by Amazon.

Better said, search the words or keywords (string of keywords – sometimes described as "Long-Tail Keywords") which readers use in order to find a medical thriller. Try to avoid single words, rather use keyword strings! As you know from your own searches: consumers don't search with single words.

Edit, Edit, and Edit Even More!

Recently I read a fantastic book, which really hooked me, wanting to read more from this author. It had not a single typo or grammar error. However, the protagonist, a young girl, was using an iPod, later in the story she was getting tickets to a concert that actually happened in the late 60's and when she went missing, her mother gave the girl's birth date as in 1948 to the police. This really great book lacked a good editor to point out these errors.

Some editors work only on the structural and line level. Others also copy edit, or specialize in copy editing alone. Don't forget to get your blurb edited, too! Before you hire an editor, you need to know what kind of help you're looking for. Some editors work only on the structural and line level. Others also copy edit or specialize in copy editing alone.

Services That Editors Will Perform Include:

- suggesting cutting out characters
- changing or omitting dialogue
- changing the narrative arc of the novel
- moving chapters around
- giving other suggestions that will improve the book

Developmental Edit

Do you need "big-picture" feedback about structure, style, pacing, and voice? A developmental edit for a work of nonfiction may include feedback about the book's organizational structure as well as both stylistic and informational strengths and weaknesses. For fiction manuscripts, developmental editing also includes notes on plot, a point of view and characterization. Often, this edit is given in the form of a detailed report or letter rather than as notes made directly on the manuscript.

Line Edit

In a line edit, your editor will point out specific things that don't sound convincing, such as certain lines of dialogue, or pacing problems in a given section.

Copy Editing and Proofreading

These are about fixing errors in grammar, punctuation, spelling, word choice and sentence structure as well as catching continuity issues.

Proofreading

It means typos, repeated words, spelling, punctuation and formatting issues (how things look on a page) as they occur in your book's final environment. If your book will be printed, your editor will proofread a PDF. Proofreading is the last pair of eyes on your book before it goes live, the last chance to catch an error before a reader finds it and gleefully points it out.

Edit, Edit, And Edit Even More!

Many self-publishing authors dread the costly editing process. This is a big mistake, as it might cost you not only readers but your reputation as a writer. Sure, one of the highest expenses in book productions is the editing process. But there are ways to reduce these costs, especially if you use editors that charge by the hour instead of by the word.

Let several other writers (beta readers) read your manuscript. They might see inconsistencies in the flow of your writing, or major grammatical errors and typos. In order to get a more impartial view of your story before you submit to an editor, you can also join a reader community website, such as *Wattpad.com* – http://wattpad.com/ – or *LibraryThing.com* – http://librarything.com/ – to get a range of readers opinions.

To save editing cost, use of these great – often free – online tools that are available these days:

- *Edit Minion* – http://editminion.com/ – This free software identifies adverbs, passive voice, duplicate or frequently used words, and sentence length

- *Language Tool* – https://languagetool.org/ – A tool that is capable of proofreading more than 20 languages. Style issues will be marked in blue

- *Paper Rater* – https://www.paperrater.com/ –Robust grammar checking tool which allows you to find those pesky mistakes and correct them

My advice is to not use only ONE software, but at least TWO – better THREE – and use them in separate sessions to fine comb your manuscript BEFORE sending it to a professional editor.

Why You Still Need an Editor:

Pre-editing will save you money and embarrassment. However, none of these grammar tools can replace human intelligence. You will still need a professional editor who then fine-tunes your manuscript for an outstanding, successful book.

Increase Readership: Create an Audiobook

Re-purpose your manuscript and make more out of it than just a book and an e-book. Why don't you also create an audiobook from your novel, or even from non-fiction? Audiobooks are becoming more and more popular!

Your readers can listen to your audiobooks, which can easily double their book consumption. This is due to the fact that they are using the time that previously was not available and turning it into valuable "reading" time. They can listen in the car, bus, train, plane. Or while exercising, walking or hiking, on the beach, or while doing mundane tasks around the house or yard. Special needs readers, such as blind ones, will have access to your written words in the form of an audiobook. Audiobooks can be listened to on the following devices: iPod, SmartPhone, or other MP3 players, even on most e-readers, such as Kindle and Nook.

There are several ways of producing an audiobook:

- You can use ACX (owned by Amazon) who produce your audiobook for free. But they will split all proceeds in half once the audiobook sells.

Find all the details at their *website – https://www.acx.com/*.

- Aggregator *Draft2Digital – https://draft2digital.com/* – is in a partnership with *FindawayVoices – https://findawayvoices.com/*, an audiobook creation and distribution service which gives authors more freedom and control over their work. Authors keep 80 percent of all royalties earned through the sale of recordings. Audiobooks are created and sold to listeners in more than 170 countries via the world's largest audiobook distribution network.

- FindawayVoices is an innovator in the audiobook industry for more than 10 years and a global leader in digital content delivery across retail, library, and K–12 channels. FindawayVoices works with you to make the right decisions when creating your audiobooks. They provide a list of suggested narrators at a range of PFH rates. This lets you choose the right voice at the right price. The range is typical $150 to $400 per finished hour. See a *table on their website – https://findawayvoices.com/pricing/* – to better estimate your potential audiobook investment.

- Do it all yourself. If you are on a very tight budget, and you have a professional voice, you can make audiobooks with some relatively inexpensive equipment.

- Hire a professional narrator who specializes in audiobooks. This person will receive a percentage of the royalty after production of your audiobook.

- Organize a professional production (costly!) and keep all your royalties for yourself.

A membership at *www.Audible.com* – *http://www.audible.com/* – (owned by Amazon.com) is a good deal for your readers. They can choose from various plans, and easily download digital audiobooks to their preferred device. Your readers can also go to their local public library to get audiobooks for free. For more information about audiobook production, links and addresses, please see this *blog post* – *http://savvybookwriters.wordpress.com/2013/09/30/how-else-can-you-leverage-your-manuscript*.

A Print Version of Your Book – Will it Sell More Copies?

Why should you have a print book, such as a paperback, and not go with only the digital version? There are many reasons:

- You can hand out review copies to newspaper/magazine or book blog reviewers

- Half of all book buyers still choose printed books at the moment

- Local media/TV interviewers who host you will want to show a copy of your book

- You can sell your book easier to libraries

- You need a print version of your book to participate in a Goodreads giveaway

- Some people don't own, or want to own, an e-reader or they just love paper books

- If you write non-fiction, it is almost a must to offer it in paper as well
- A print book requires an ISBN number, which can be listed with Bowker at worldwide bookstores
- Physical books are just nicer to give on Christmas, unless you put an e-book on a new e-reader – both as a Holiday gift
- You can sell more e-books because they seem to cost so much less in comparison to print books!
- You can list your book in more categories/genres on Amazon. You are allowed to choose two categories/genres per book type. If you have two print and two digital versions, it will increase your book's visibility. You will also be able to see exactly in which genre you have the most success.

Amazon Giveaways

Well, their giveaways are maybe not as popular and well-known as Goodreads Giveaways among author-publishers. Other enterprises at Amazon seem to use it a lot – mainly to receive favorable reviews of their products. Giveaway contests are an excellent way for authors to drum up some buzz for their book. Especially as Amazon does all the product shipping – which has its drawbacks as you will never know who is the recipient. With Goodreads print book Giveaways you do the shipping, but on the other hand you know who is the lucky winner – and hopefully reader and reviewer of your book. At least you can add a nice card to your book, mentioning your additional titles and links to your social media site, inviting them to follow you. Sorry, but

Giveaways via Amazon are only open to legal residents of the U.S.A, 18 or older. Get here all the information about *Amazon's Giveaways – https://www.amazon.com/gp/giveaway/home*.

Get an ISBN Number and Register Your Copyright

ISBN is the International Standard Book Number, a 13-digit number that uniquely identifies books published anywhere in the world. Selling your e-book on Amazon doesn't necessarily mean you need an ISBN. You will automatically get an ASIN, Amazon's identifier. Other retailers, such as Kobo, may require an ISBN. In Italy (maybe in some other countries too) books without an ISBN are not considered books, but rather digital products and are five times higher taxed than print books – not attractive for book purchasers.

ISBN numbers are assigned by a group of worldwide agencies coordinated by the International *ISBN Agency – http://savvybookwriters.wordpress.com/2012/01/30/isbn-numbers-and-how-to-get-one* – in London, England. In the United States, ISBN's are assigned by the ISBN Agency Bowker, which is the independent agent for this system. You can apply for an ISBN online. On average, it takes about two weeks for ISBN's to be assigned. Good news for Canadian writers: ISBN are free there, you order them online and get the number right away.

IMPORTANT: Getting your own ISBN is crucial because the initial purchaser of this number is considered to be the official publisher. Don't fall for a "free" ISBN, and don't purchase it from other sources than the *official organizations* – <u>http://savvybookwriters.wordpress.com/2012/06/08/author-beware-unauthorized-resellers-of-isbns</u>.

Why do you Need a Copyright Registration?

It is not required for an author to register your work or even provide a notice; but, there are reasons to protect yourself and what you created. For one thing, proving ownership of your work may be a difficult matter without proper evidence. Often, it boils down to a case of "their word against yours". Without proper protection, work that you have created could end up making money for someone else. Addresses for registering your copyright can be found *here* – <u>http://savvybookwriters.wordpress.com/2012/01/28/why-should-you-register-the-copyright-of-your-manuscript</u>.

List Your Book Worldwide

Few authors have ever heard of *BowkerLink* – <u>http://www.bowkerlink.com/corrections/common/home.asp</u>. It is a source for publishers and distributors seeking to update, or add to, title listings found in *Books in Print*, *Global Books In Print*, and the *Publisher Authority Database*. How can readers, bookstores, or librarians in Japan, Australia, the UK, or Belize find your book and read, buy or lend it? *Books in Print* helps you search the marketplace, find the right titles, and explore all known format options, including e-Book sources. Listing your book worldwide through BowkerLink is totally free for authors and publishers.

Create Excitement With a Book Cover Poll

Try to engage your potential readers early on. Polls and surveys add an element of fun to the conversation. People love to take surveys. It will build community engagement, real relationships and interest. It will also leave readers more receptive to your next book promotion. With simple online surveys you can take your social media networking success to an entirely new level.

Invite your networks to provide honest and immediate feedback. For example, ask members to choose which of (at least three) book covers they like best and share their thoughts about the design. You can also let them choose the name of your protagonist, or which online retailers should carry your book, among other things. Include an incentive to encourage your followers to complete your survey. For example, the winner of the most popular book cover chosen could win a Kindle or a small digital camera.

SurveyMonkey.com – *https://www.surveymonkey.com/mp/social-media-surveys* – has a free, basic poll version. *SodaHead.com* – *https://www.sodahead.com/widget/create* – has one as well. *TWTPoll.com* – *http://twtpoll.com/home/tour* – has a pay-as-you-go version for $7 per survey. Get lots of practical tips on *SocialMediaExaminer* – *http://www.socialmediaexaminer.com/online-surveys* – on how to incorporate your poll at a variety of social media sites.

Gather as Many Early Reviews as Possible

Be aware that big media reviewers do not even accept 10% of the submissions they receive. As an independent author, you are competing with traditional publishers. However, if you don't give it a try and send in a professional query, you will never know. Book review editors are not the only ones who might accept your books for review.

You can try columnists as well, especially if you write non-fiction. For example, if your book is about an adventurous bike tour in Jamaica, you can send your review submission to both the travel section editor of a major newspaper as well as the sports editor.

Always check their submission rules carefully! Most review sites want hard copies of the book at least 3 months prior to publication. Even if you have planned to publish an e-book, get 30-50 copies printed at a digital printer, or at CreateSpace. You can also use any of the new Espresso-Publishing machines that you can find in major cities. They deliver via mail or UPS. Print copies are not only important for reviewers, but also for your book launch or book signings. They are also useful to sell to people who prefer print instead of e-books. Other reviewers, especially top book bloggers, accept books after their release, and more and more reviewers now accept e-books.

Create an address database, or any kind of list, where you type in the following information: title, name, address, and email of the recipient, date of submission, and their guidelines. Never, ever send your review query "to the editor" or "to whom it may concern…" Verify that they review your genre of the book before you submit. Follow their publication-date deadlines.

When Should You Send Out Your Review Submission?

Submit your query in January/February for spring and July/August for fall, if you want less competition from major publishers. Don't send out your query to arrive at the editor's office on a Monday. Time it to reach the appropriate editor on a Thursday or Friday.

Make sure that you include all your contact information: name, mailing address, website address, phone number, and email address. Use *http://about.me* to create an appealing information site about yourself and include it in your contact information.

> IMPORTANT: Don't forget to include the book's information: price, ISBN number, number of pages, and genre. Carefully pack your book in airfoil envelopes or boxes. You want them to look professional and brand new when they arrive at the editor's office.

Add a media kit, including your biography as well as professional images in high-resolution and in several sizes. In an e-mail, you can include a book trailer link, a blurb, the synopsis of the book, and your contact information.

Some of the Most Reputable Reviewers – Read by Bookstore Owners and Librarians:

- Los Angeles Reviews
- Armchair Reviews
- ForeWord Reviews

- Library Journal
- Midwest Book Review
- NY Times Reviews
- Indie Reader
- USA TODAY

Paid Reviews:
- Kirkus
- Publishers Weekly
- US Book Reviews

Don't forget to send a thank-you note/e-mail to anyone who reviews your book. They took a long time reading and reviewing your work, writing an article, and getting back to you. So, take five minutes and write them a thank-you letter or email!

Advance Book Reviews

Learn from trade publishers how to prepare for a book launch. The worst error a self-publishing author can make is to expedite the book's launch. Plan well ahead and try to get as many credible reviews as possible by way of sending out "Advance Review Copies".

Did you ever wonder why brand new books already have reviews? New author-publishers can learn a lot in bookstores. Check out how professionally published books look. Many of these trade books have either on their back cover (paperback) or on the binding flap (hardcover) several snippets of the book reviews, as well as endorsements from bestselling writers or other professionals. These were already written before the book was printed.

Traditional publishers may budget anywhere from fifty to several hundred "free and review" copies. Advance Review Copies (ARC's) are what they send out six months (!) ahead of the book launch date. ARC's are produced by publishers and distributed to booksellers and journalists prior to the official release date.

Because ARCs may not have been put through the entire editing process, the copy will often differ slightly from the standard edition of the book. Important: always label the ARCs with one of the following phrases: "Uncorrected Proof" "Advance Reading Copy", "Uncorrected Advance Copy", or "Not for Sale". Learn more about *how to prepare for these reviews* – http://savvybookwriters.wordpress.com/2013/08/01/how-to-prepare-your-book-for-reviews.

How these pre-edition galleys are produced, and to whom they should be sent, is explained in "*How to Get Reviews Before Your Books Launch*" – http://savvybookwriters.wordpress.com/2013/12/12/how-to-get-reviews-before-your-books-launch. Prepare your book review query well in advance and learn what to avoid when *pitching to reviewers*. – http://www.booklifenow.com/2009/12/critics-on-rookie-mistakes-and-how-to-avoid-them-when-submitting-your-book-for-review.

The more work you do to promote your book before the

publication date, the more people will already know about it. This means more book sales!

Get Pre-Orders For Your New Book

Is your book launch within the next 3 months? Amazon allows you to make your new books available for pre-order in Kindle online stores worldwide. With a few quick and easy steps you can create a pre-order page up to 90 days in advance of your book's release date. Amazon promises to set up your pre-order product page within 24 hours. When you make your book available for pre-order, your readers can order the book anytime leading up to the release date you set. Amazon delivers your book to your pre-order customers on your book's launch date.

Amazon explains: "You will list your book as you would with any other KDP book. When you are adding a new book, you will come to step 4 ("Select Your Book Release Option"). Choose "Make my book available for pre-order", and set a date in the future. That's it!" Do you have more questions? *Here are the answers – https://kdp.amazon.com/help?topicId=A3P7F81795P0RA&ref_=pe_445910_119439090_3.*

Pre-Orders on Apple iBooks

Sure, Amazon sells the most ebooks, but did you know that Apple has moved past Barnes & Noble into the number two position, and is continuing to grow? You can publish directly on iBooks if you're a Mac user, or you can take advantage of all the same opportunities by publishing through aggregators/book distributors. Some authors even make more money from iBooks than they do from Amazon.

Use iBook Pre-orders and Promote it to Readers

You can add iBooks up to a year in advance. Having it there for so long means that as soon as someone finishes a book, they can order the next one with no need to remember buying it later.

Pre-orders on iBooks rank twice. They are counted in the iBooks bestseller lists while on pre-order and then you get the sales counted all on the live date. Yes, you have to do more planning in advance, but it helps to keep to the production schedule and customers know what to expect next.

Promote your book while it is on pre-order. Drive customers to the pre-order site by revealing aspects during the journey to publication. Do a cover reveal a few months out and an early sample of your book. The pre-order, if it's a series, it will be linked on the iBooks page.

Get Pre-Orders on Your Website

Establishing a pre-order page on Amazon is not the only way to create excitement for your new book. Set up a special page on your website and blog so that readers can order your book ahead of the launch. Offer them an incentive when ordering directly from you, such as a free short story, which you can email them right away.

After all, you earn more money when people come to your website for book purchases than from Amazon orders. This fact is even more important: you will have all the reader data, which you will never receive from Amazon! Offer the paper book, signed, as a pre-order at an attractive price. Remember to include the cost of shipping. You will have to pay shipping the copies to your place before you ship them out yourself. Much easier: you can order them for your customer and let it ship as a gift from you. This way you save yourself time and higher postage. Promote this pre-order sale through your e-mail newsletter to friends, followers and readers, and on all your social media sites.

How to Deal With the Media and Book Bloggers

In order to get the word out about the upcoming book launch and to receive positive feedback – from articles in newspapers, magazines, and book blogs, as well as from interviews – writers should deal professionally with anyone who could tout their book. Which doesn't relate to only the national press and TV. Often, book bloggers can do more than newspapers to help your book get discovered. After all, they have the right audience. Don't be surprised when you never get an answer to your press releases, if you don't convince the journalist or interviewer that their listeners and readers can profit from your information. Here are a few tips:

Rule # 1: Build relationships months in advance of pitching! Mostly via social media. This way the editor knows already your name and maybe has seen your posts or comments.

- Have a press page on your website
- Offer a variety of cover photos
- Give lots of information about you and your book
- Have a (virtual) portfolio
- Don't forget to follow up
- Be prepared anytime for one-on-one interviews
- Become familiar with the media outlet

Get more tips in this article: *7 Errors To Avoid When Dealing With the Media*. – http://savvybookwriters.wordpress.com/2013/01/27/7-errors-writers-make-when-dealing-with-the-media.

Many writers dream of the exposure their book could receive in print and online articles, or on a popular radio or TV show. In reality, this is merely one more step in your book public relations (PR) efforts, not the start of a million book sales avalanche. Rather, see it as an opportunity to possibly get a free video recording of your interview or another article for your book's portfolio. It also increases your recognition as an author, and it's a great sales argument when dealing with libraries or bookstores. Don't forget: Public Relation (PR) and book marketing are long-term strategies!

Create a Media Kit

"Microsoft Publisher" software is all you need to make a professional press kit to send out to the right newspaper and magazine editors, radio and TV journalists, or agents. Include in your writing the market research you have done to show how numerous readers could profit from your new book. Include the best bits of material from your work; don't forget a link to your book trailer. Always send this kit to the editor with his or her name on it. A bit of research is necessary to set up a list of current recipients. A cornucopia of tips can be found in this article by *Joel Friedlander* – *http://www.thebookdesigner.com/*.

Submit Photos of Your Book Cover

You know Flickr as a photo storing and sharing site, but did you know you can use it to market your book there? You can't use it to advertise; this would be against their terms of use, and they would block your account. However, there is a subtle way to introduce your book on photo-sharing sites, comparable to showing your book. This includes illustrations from the inside of your book or images from the area your story takes place.

Start by commenting regularly on Flickr. Tell people what you like about their images. Be encouraging and invite people to the Flickr groups you have joined. Embed links to your Flickr site in photos you use on blogs. Share your link on social media sites, such as: Twitter, Google+, Pinterest, Facebook, Instagram, and Goodreads. This action will draw visitors from third-party sites to your Flickr page. For instance, Pinterest has recently made a feature that allows sharing from Flickr. It automatically shows proper credit and a link back to the original photographer. There are no longer any copyright and fair-use problems.

Tagging and grouping photos: You can use up to 75 tags to describe your photo of the book cover, more than Amazon, or any other page, allows 75 tags! That's a lot of possibilities to let people know about your book! Organize your work into collections on your profile page. Group them based on common themes, formats, or any other elements. Don't forget to add notes to explain or comment on your photo. In other words, you will be *mentioning your book – http://savvybookwriters.wordpress.com/2012/08/16/how-to-market-your-book-on-photo-sites*.

If you want to see your images gain a wider audience, start offering a few of them for fair use. This especially includes your book cover photo or snippets of the cover image. Blogs and sharing sites are always on the lookout for royalty-free images they can use.

For only $25 you get a professional account on Flickr. You will receive an official icon showing that you are a professional user, which actually adds more credibility in the community. You also get enhanced features, such as unlimited photos as well as video or HD video capabilities. If you have a professional account on Flickr, you are allowed to post a photo in up to sixty user group pools! Free accounts only allow you to put each photo in ten user groups. Flickr is not the only site where you can show images of your book and its topics. Consider Pinterest, Instagram, PhotoBucket, or PhotoLog. Find a great overview of all the photo sharing sites, including details, such as membership numbers here on this *Wikipedia* site: *http://en.wikipedia.org/wiki/List_of_photo-sharing_websites*.

Book Cover Design Award

For years "*The Book Designer*", Joel Friedlander, – *http://www.thebookdesigner.com/* – a book layout specialist, has offered a monthly book cover design competition for already published books with a sales link: *The Cover Design Awards*. Why should you participate?

- It attracts links from book blogs, which will want to connect with the winners
- You can write about it if you win a popular contest
- You might gain more readers if your book belongs to the "winners"
- You can find more great designers and indie authors

Joel Friedlander – *http://helpareporter.com/* – has looked at so many books over the years he can tell the ones that work from those that don't. Before you submit your work, check out the design award pages from previous months. Read also his submission rules.

Get Help From Journalists

Are you a non-fiction writer? Then sign up on *HelpaReporter.com* – *http://helpareporter.com/* – (HARO). Several email lists are sent out on a daily basis, full of reporters needing experts for stories. Search for those that fall within your expertise and publications with smaller and more targeted readerships, such as local weekly publications.

These media outlets are often run by just two or three people. They do accept guest columns or articles because it will save them the time of tracking down a story on their own. You might get wonderful (and often paid) opportunities to write and include a byline about your work, including links to your site. This is one more chance to promote your books!

How to Get Help from Freelance Journalists

Joan Stewart writes in her article "here are the top three reasons why they are such *powerful media contacts*: – *https://www.thebookdesigner.com/2017/12/how-to-use-freelance-journalists-in-a-book-publicity-campaign/*:

1. They're familiar with online and print media that buy articles and reviews. Full-time or part-time freelance journalists – especially those who rely on writing to make a living – know far more than you ever will about the wide variety of online and offline news outlets, websites, newspapers, magazines, and newsletters.

2. You don't have to worry about pitching a story to a busy journalist. The freelancer pitches it. Emailing or talking to journalists can be intimidating. Not so much with freelancers who are always open to ideas that will make compelling stories they can sell.

3. A freelance journalist can use your knowledge as a source for multiple stories sold to different media outlets.

4. Let's say you're a cookbook author, and a freelancer uses you as a source for a story she's writing for

Eating Well magazine. If she likes working with you, and she knows you are a helpful source, she might return to you again and again for stories she's selling to Cooking Light, Clean Eating or Plate magazine."

PART FOUR

In this chapter, you will receive tips for "passive marketing"; book layout tips, your author pages, and other places you can sell your book besides the major online retailers.

Find Marketing Steps Inside of Your Book
Book Promotion: Leverage Your e-Book Layout

Traditionally, the first page of print books is set up according to the Chicago Manual of Style. The front matter pages get lowercase Roman numerals instead of regular Arabic page numbers. However, that only applies to print books, digital books don't use page numbers. The book's first pages are set up in this sequence:

- half-title page
- series title
- title page
- copyright page
- dedications
- a quote or epigraph
- Table of Contents (TOC)
- list of illustrations

- list of tables
- the foreword
- preface
- acknowledgments
- introduction

Only the title page and copyright page are mandatory; this is the same for e-books. Read more about print book layout here in this *blog article – http://savvybookwriters.wordpress.com/2014/09/11/7-book-layout-errors-you-will-want-to-avoid*.

"Look Inside"

When people use the "Look Inside" feature, especially in e-books, those traditional front matter/first book pages could easily take up half of the feature space. That's why you will want to move everything but the title page, copyright page, and the Table of Contents (TOC) to the last pages of the book.

Copyright

The copyright page is essential because many e-book retailers won't accept an e-book for sale unless it includes the copyright page. It should consist of: Copyright (Year) Author name. For example, it could read either "Copyright 2012 Allen Miller", or "© 2012 Allen Miller". Quite a bit of the content in a printed book's copyright page is irrelevant to an e-book.

Table of Contents (TOC)

Chapter entries in the content listing should be hyperlinked so that users can go straight to the start of a chapter from the TOC. Distributors such as Amazon will insist that you do this, or they won't accept your e-book. It improves the quality and usability of your e-book. Don't include page numbers from your printed edition; it doesn't make sense in an e-book. Due to the fact that there are a variety of e-Readers, tablets, and even computer screens on which e-books are read (and even more due to the font size an e-book reader may choose), page numbers are useless.

Take Advantage of Hyperlinks

An e-book is simply a specialized web page. Capitalize on this fact for some "free advertising" of your other books and your social media sites. E-books can also be used to gather email newsletter sign-ups and book reviews. Set up the following pages right after the book's last page:

- Review Links: Give your readers a reason to leave positive reviews and recommend the book to others. Once readers have finished the last page and liked your book, they are more likely to leave an immediate book review.

- Set up an opt-in link for your newsletter mailing list

- Link also to all your Social Media sites

- Amazon author page and all your book online retailers

- GoodReads.com and other book communities

- Your own website and blog
- Google+
- LinkedIn
- Twitter.com
- Pinterest
- Goodreads

You may have buttons already set up for Google+, Twitter, Goodreads, and so forth. Just click on them, copy the URL out of the address bar on the bottom of your page, and create the link.

Make it Easy for Reviewers

Amazon uses its own identifier for e-books, ASIN, which means you have to wait until after the book is definitely published in the Kindle Store to create a link. As soon as your book is uploaded, you can use your book's Amazon page and link to "*Post your own review*" – *http://www.amazon.com/your-title-ebook/dp/B00000ABC*.

Building these links is just a matter of copying and pasting. If you are not familiar with HTML, ask your e-book formatter or web designer to do it. It's worth the small effort. In addition, it's a great chance to make the next sale, get reviews, new fans who rave about your book, and followers on your social media sites. You can certainly use logos or sharing buttons in your e-book content. *This process is described* – *http://www.thebookdesigner.com/2013/08/david-kudler-kindle* – by David Kudler for HTML-based ePub files.

Retweet Buttons

People are naturally inclined to share content they find valuable. It shows their followers that they are someone worth following because of the useful information they share. This makes them a valuable contributor to the social networks. Encouraging your readers to share your book's content in social media also extends the reach of it to people outside of your direct network.

A special retweet button allows any reader to easily post a tweet into his or her Twitter account. Also, it's not just any tweet; it's prefabricated by you and it links back to your e-book. It links back to the original landing page where your document resides. You can place it in your website, blog or book manuscript. Set up the retweet image in more than one location of your future book.

- Where do you want to send readers? You certainly want to send them to your book's sales page!

- Use a link shortener, such as *bit.ly* – *http://bit.ly/* – as the original Amazon link is too long

- Create a short recommendation text to accompany the link

- Avoid hashtags, or replace them with "%23". For example, instead of "#reading" use "%23reading"

- Acrobat Pro will allow you to create hot-links inside your e-book file

- Use the "Link Tool" in Acrobat Pro (under the advance editing menu). Locate the retweet buttons you added into your file and create a clickable link for each retweet graphic

- To keep the link type invisible, highlight style to 'None' and select 'Open a web page' as the link action
- Then, hit the 'Next' button. You will be prompted to enter your special URL
- Now, repeat the process for all the retweet buttons you have in your e-book manuscript

More tips, including how to do it in InDesign, can be found *in this article – https://digitalfireflymarketing.com/sharing-ebooks-hyperlinks-indesign* – by Marissa Treece.

Another option is to use *Twitter's ClicktoTweet – http://clicktotweet.com/* – version which is even easier to use: Just type in your text, get the code, copy, and place it into your book's manuscript, blog or on the website or any social media page. You can use their free version, which includes an image of the Twitter logo, or if you go with the paid one, you may use your own logo or a thumbnail of your book's cover for the message (one more reason to keep your cover image and the font very clear and easy to read as this logo is tiny).

The Last Pages of Your Book

Once you have created all these URL's, you may then add these pages to the end of the book:

- List of your previous books with sales page URL's
- Acknowledgments
- "About the author" or biography
- Bibliography

- Index Links (for non-fiction books)

Setting up your book layout in the same professional way as trade publishers do. And in addition incorporate valuable links, retweet buttons, sign-up forms for your email newsletter and – most important – review encouragements in your digital version of the book. It will bring you many more new readers for your books!

Choose the Right Book Category/Genre

It can make all the difference in how well your book sells. Readers have to FIND your book to buy it. When I consult with clients and check out their online sales pages, I often find that they choose only one category. They could select two (or even six) categories, if their work is available in print, audio and digital. Sometimes they don't even bother to choose a category at all.

Why are the proper categories so important, for example on Amazon? Let's look at *NEVER SAY SORRY* – *http://bit.ly/Y6ABT*, a thriller that runs the gamut from corporate ethics, law, medical treatments for cancer, and hedge funds:

The competition for this title in the e-Book category follows:

Thrillers (The book's competition is 112,518 other books; this is where it was initially posted.)

Fiction > Mystery & Thrillers >Thrillers > Medical (The competition is only 394 books.)

Fiction > Mystery & Thrillers >Thrillers> Legal (The competition is only 1,303 books.)

The author can choose both categories for her e-book, medical and legal thriller. If she leaves book listed only under thriller, she will compromise its ranking tremendously. This could almost kill the book.

IMPORTANT: If you don't choose the right categories, you may never become a category bestseller and never gain the publicity needed for higher visibility. In addition, you may never be recognized by Amazon's algorithms, which gives you better rankings in the numerous other Amazon Top 100 lists. This, in turn, means higher visibility for your books.

Millions of books are being published in the world today. Categorization of books by topic and content has become an important tool for readers to enable them to choose what they want to read. Readers, booksellers, publishers, and authors all benefit from category descriptions for books. It is immensely important for authors to determine the best genre or category to identify their book before publishing. A comprehensive listing of genres can be found *in this blog post – http://savvybookwriters.wordpress.com/2013/06/03/how-to-choose-the-right-genre-for-your-book*.

Let Your Readers Pay With a Tweet

Use social media to let your new book go viral via Twitter by re-tweeting to your customers' friends and followers. Nowadays, it's sometimes more valuable to have people talking about your book than to have the money you would earn from it.

Sell Your Free Book for the Price of a Tweet

Pay-with-a-Tweet is a service that allows visitors access your content (e-book, video or song) without having to "pay" for it by giving up any personal information on a form. All they have to do is share it with their own networks on Twitter, LinkedIn, or on Google+. Three steps are all it takes to get your book noticed:

- Step 1: Create a button and embed it on your website, prequel, blog or e-mail
- Step 2: Users access your content and 'post' about it
- Step 3: Your users' shares are re-tweeted and re-posted by their friends and followers

It's Easy to Set Up and Use!

Not only is the tool super easy for your landing page visitors to use, it's also quite easy to set up. *Pay-With-A-Tweet – http://www.paywithatweet.com/* – allows you to stash content (a song or an e-book) and only allows access to it after a user has tweeted something about it. In other words, it's like a paywall in which you pay by tweeting about something. If it's true that attention is a scarce resource, drawing attention to something ought to be worth something, right? Read more on this *blog article*: – *http://savvybookwriters.wordpress.com/2014/04/10/pay-with-a-tweet-and-how-it-works.*

Here are the benefits: you don't need to keep your book exclusive on Amazon Select. Every free download creates buzz. You don't have to sign up or pay for advertising and it has a good chance to go viral.

Press Releases for a Review – Are They Worth the Effort?

Short answer: only if you are lucky. This is what press release companies will NOT tell you: Usually, book editors will not review a book that is not published in hardback or is self-published. A trade paperback is also a huge strike against the chances of the book getting reviewed. But, it doesn't make your chances absolutely impossible. Even though first-time author books are seldom reviewed. Non-fiction books seem a little more likely to entice reviews from them. If you really want to gamble on this, do it yourself (DIY) instead of wasting your money. So, how can you find these editors/journalists?

Nothing could be easier: just google "Newspaper Book Review Editors". On one of the top-ranking places you will find John Kremer's generous and helpful free listing of editors of leading newspapers in the USA. Authors from other parts of the world just need to add the name of their country into the search function. This doesn't mean that editors wouldn't write about English books from abroad. But the likelihood is higher when the author comes from the same country.

How to Use an Excel List and More Tips

John Kremer – http://www.bookmarket.com/ – also shows how a professional list of editors could be compiled in the

Window's Excel program. His lists are a free service and updated constantly! As editors often change or retire, it is necessary to call ahead before you send out your news release. John Kremer also cautions: "Note that most newspaper book reviewers are only interested in major fiction, major social issue books, biographies of famous people, and some regional books."

Other ways to find names of media professionals who could introduce your book to a wider audience include reading reviews in magazines and newspapers (online and print) and listening to radio interviews. Note the name of the editor, journalist, reporter, or interviewer. Google the mail or e-mail information and contact the appropriate person. Sometimes, names can also be found on new books' back cover blurbs. Look also on the LinkedIn search function for editors and journalist in your genre.

> IMPORTANT: The very best way to get your foot in the door is to write articles and features for major newspapers and magazines; you are allowed a short bio and a link to your author website. Other amenities include: you can network with your colleagues and if the review editor likes your book, she or he might review it. If you get a really great review: copy it, place it on your website, link to it as well as post and tweet it to gain the maximum exposure. Yes, and show your gratitude by thanking the reviewer.

Create a Separate BOOK PAGE or AUTHOR PAGE

Once your book goes live on Amazon, you are eligible for an Amazon Author Central Account – and your very own author web page on Amazon! Best of all: there will be no advertising on your site. It will contain only a large image of your book(s), your reviews, and your book's description. Not only will your Amazon website get a high page ranking – Author Central tools are effective in marketing your books and promoting yourself as an author. Use your Author Central page to provide more information for your readers, such as upcoming events, a complete listing of your books, more images and videos, your book trailer, and even excerpts from your blog.

Here are some tips:

- Add a professional author photo and biography
- Add all your books
- Include videos (e.g. trailers for your books)
- Add up to seven additional photos of you writing your books or scenes from your book
- Add images or graphics from your book's content
- Write a biography; make sure to update it frequently
- List events, such as book readings or book launches
- Add your Twitter address so that people can see your latest tweet and easily follow you
- Set up the "Search Inside/Look Inside" feature
- Add an RSS feed, which will link your blog to your page. This is a great way to get your blog in front of new readers and encourage them to follow you.

- Edit your product description and "about the author" section. Add any professional reviews you have received so far
- View and edit the list of books you have written because the Amazon system doesn't always get it right. If you have written more than one book, it will link your titles together. This will allow your readers to find all of your work.

More on *Amazon's Central help site*.
https://authorcentral.amazon.com/gp/help?topicID=200649520

You need separate accounts, for the UK, CA and US versions of Amazon. Create the author page for each country separately. However, it is just a matter of copy and paste. Try to create your foreign country pages in their language. Either via Google translation or even better, ask a native speaker of the language for which you need the short text. Use the Amazon Central account separately for each country. For example:

Amazon Author Central UK:
http://authorcentral.amazon.co.uk

Amazon Author Central US:
http://authorcentral.amazon.com

Amazon Author Central Canada:
http://authorcentral.amazon.ca

Author Page at D2D

Authors need to have their books easily found by potential readers. It is one of the primary goals of marketing, and for authors. It can be the difference between having a hobby and having a career. Author pages at D2D include:

- Your author bio
- Your author photo
- Links to your social media accounts
- Customizable page elements to help promote your book to readers
- A button to follow you for new release notifications or to join your mailing list
- Carousels of your books and series, so readers can easily find your work!

Read more about *D2D author pages* – *http://www.savvybookwriters.com/new-author-pages-on-d2d-plus-more-goodies/* – and see an *example* – *https://www.books2read.com/ap/n4EYY8/Doris-Maria-Heilmann.*

Books2Read is the home of one of their favorite book marketing tools: Universal Book Links (UBLs). Universal Links are a single web page/URL that you can share and which will send your excited prospective reader to the store of their choice.

The Goodreads Author Program

Use it to promote yourself and your books. It is a completely free feature designed to help authors reach their target audience: passionate readers. This is the perfect place for new and established authors to promote their books. This is an excerpt what can you can do as an author at Goodreads:

- Show Your Author Profile
- Add a picture, a bio, and post videos
- Share your list of favorite books and recent reads with your fans!
- Write a blog and generate a band of followers
- Publicize upcoming events, such as book signings and speaking engagements
- Share book excerpts and other writing
- Write a quiz about your book or a related topic
- Add the Goodreads Author widget to your personal website or blog to show off reviews of your books

Your Google+ Book Page

To help build the most efficient and awesome Google+ page for your books, check out the articles compiled in a mega-list of the *top how-to guides* – *http://holykaw.alltop.com/mega-list-of-how-to-guides-for-google-brand-p* – from around the web. How can you promote your business page? Post them on all social media sites. Don't forget: you can open a new Google+ page for each of your books.

How to Organize Your Book Launch Party

Now, you have a reason to celebrate the launch of your new book, which might have taken months or years to write: a book launch party – actual, or maybe even virtual. You will want to thank everyone who helped with the creation of your book and introduced your latest work to your dedicated readers. With today's digital printing techniques it is possible to have a couple of print books to sign at your event, even if your book is officially offered only as an e-book. Even if you don't launch a party – not even a virtual one – use some of these book marketing tips for your new work!

Plan Your Event at Least Two Months Ahead

The date can be well after the book hits the shelves, or the Amazon sales pages. What's important is that you invite as many people as possible. They won't all come, don't worry. What's also important is that you get as much buzz as possible from book bloggers, your social media followers, local book clubs, and (hopefully) the local press. Use this article as a checklist, it will give you tips in chronological order:

TWO MONTHS BEFORE THE BOOK LAUNCH:

Order Your Books in Time

Use either Amazon Publishing, any POD company, or LightningSource. You can also use an Espresso Book Machine or a local digital printer. If you go with a trade publisher, make sure you plan your event for at least two or three weeks after the first edition's date of publication. Check several times with them to make sure the books arrive at the place well ahead of your launch.

Rent a Place for Your Book Launch

Invite people for coffee or wine and cheese:

- at the Starbucks Coffee Shop, Barnes & Noble, or Chapters
- at your local library. If you expect a crowd, rent a boardroom there

You can also rent a side room in a restaurant, hotel, or museum. You may even be able to rent the foyer of a company (after working hours). The best days and times for a book launch event are Tuesday, Wednesday or Thursday between 4 pm and 8 pm.

Invite Social Media "Spreaders"

Create a "Spread the Word" page. Set up a special page on your website called "Spread the Word" in order to make it easy for people to *spread the word* – http://www.amazon.com/Training-Presentation-Skills-Business-ebook/dp/B00ACTS4A2 – via social media.

Create a short story, certainly an elaborate blog post, asking for people's help. Include some pre-made tweets that people can share with the click of a button as well as instructions on how to share the book on Google+, Twitter, Facebook, Pinterest or LinkedIn. Add several images of your book's cover, so that people can use your images by copying and pasting them into their sites.

Organize a Bloggers' Promotion

Create a blog post about why bloggers should do book reviews and include tips on how to write a professional book review. Engage them in the following manner: "Want a chance to review a new book? I am inviting up to 20 bloggers to review my new book on their blog. You will receive an extra copy that you can give away to your readers. On top of that there will be a drawing: one lucky person could win a Kindle PaperWhite or an iPad."

It should create a lot of exposure if done right. Bloggers are similar to a "new press." Also, ask people from your e-mail list (hopefully, you have one.) to participate: "I would love to get your help, spreading the word about this book launch!" and investigate ways that you can get help.

Invite the Local Press

A book launch is not necessarily a newsworthy event as millions of books are hitting the shelves every year. So, you have to find an angle to interest the press to write about it. You will also want to make readers aware of the benefit of learning about your book. Get lots of tips in this short book: *Media Training and Presentation Skills – http://www.amazon.com/Training-Presentation-Skills-Business-Profit-ebook/dp/B00ACTS4A2*.

Write an exciting press release and a separate article about your book, along with images of its cover. Start with a press page on your website. See *our blog – https://savvybookwriters.wordpress.com/2014/08/17/17-bestseller-tips-from-trade-publishers* – for instructions on how to do this. Find out the names of editors/journalists from the department that covers literature or local events. Send your invitation and information about your book to the right person. Mark your calendar to follow up after a week.

Add a Retweet Button to Your e-Book

Give away the first chapter of your book as an immediately accessible PDF on your page, or on Amazon. Include a retweet button in several strategic locations in the chapter. This allows people who love what they read to easily share with friends on Twitter. When someone clicks on the retweet button, it shows a pre-crafted tweet that says: "I'm reading @… new book: … Get the first chapter free here, too: http://…"

Ask for Book Endorsements from Influential People

Want to know how you get famous people to support your book, e-book, or blog? Well, you ask them! Some will, of course, say "no". But some will tell you "yes". You never know until you ask, right?

THREE WEEKS BEFORE YOUR LAUNCH:

Use "Event Pages".

Announce the event on Google+ and on Goodreads at least three weeks before the date. They both offer a free "Event" function, and it is easy and fast to set up. Promote this event (can be real or virtual) heavily on Twitter, Pinterest, Google+ and on your blog, as well as on your email newsletter. If your local newspaper or neighborhood paper has an event page, or if they have an online version, list your event! Search the internet for events and websites in your area and announce your book launch in these pages, too.

Print Invitations for Your Book Launch

Use your own home computer/printer to write the invitation. Include the following: a picture of your book's cover, the location and address, don't forget a map where it is located and how to get there, and the time of the event. Send your invitations out by mail or hand-deliver to those in your area. Print business cards or bookmarks as well.

Verify Delivery of Your Books

Verify that your book's delivery is on schedule, with plenty of time to arrive. Nothing is worse than having a date picked for your book release party, then having no books to sell! Reserve some copies for gifts to give to the volunteers or the host.

Get Help for the Launch Party

Get a friend or family member to assist with selling your books. You, the author, need to be free to meet and greet, mingle, market, and sign your books. Ask several people to bring their cameras and take pictures. Check your own camera and video for new batteries and a sufficient memory card. Have business cards or bookmarks to hand out as you talk with your potential buyers.

Order "Catering" for Your Launch

Organize your coffee orders, wine and cheese purchases, and water/juice. Don't forget to prepare a couple of folding chairs, tablecloth, napkins, pen and paper for notes. You may need it if someone doesn't have a card in order to write down the name and e-mail address, etc.

Order Large Posters of Your Book's Cover

The bigger the better! Get some inexpensive frames to makes them look like a valuable painting. Avoid taping them to the wall of your book launch party room; it would look cheap.

Create a Photo Contest

It can be a fun and friendly competition to get people excited about your book. There's no better platform than social media sites to do just that. For example, you can call it the "Know my Book?" or "Help Me Launch" photo contest. All participants need to do is take a creative photo with the words "Know my Book?" or "Help Me Launch." The three best images might receive the book, or you can offer an additional first prize of an e-reader or a digital camera.

Prepare an 'Event" Web Page

In order to upload images and videos from your book launch and to introduce your book via a short video (don't forget to add purchase links!) set up an extra page on your website. You can even set up an extra blog. This URL can later be used to blog or post about the event. Don't stop promoting your book launch several times a day on Twitter, Google+, Pinterest or Flickr with a variety of photos or a book trailer. You should also promote it to your e-mail list.

Broadcast Live Videos

In order to promote the event party, talk about subjects related to the book – but do not overtly pitch the book! Organize and let someone connect with Google+

Hangouts to show the event in real time. Double check that the person can do both of the following in a professional manner: Take several short videos from an event similar to your upcoming book launch and set up the "Hangout" on your computer. Make sure you have WiFi at this location.

DAY OF THE EVENT

Come Early! Check your equipment and the internet connection once more a day before, or on the morning of the event. Set up tables and chairs, if possible, and hang up your book's images. On the big day, you should plan to do the following: come an hour or more before you expect your first guests to place your books, decorations, and catering.

Gather Email Addresses From Visitors

You want to stay in touch with people you spend time with at your launch party. Make sure you have a way to capture each attendee's email address in one of the following ways: a sign-up sheet, a bowl for business cards, or a laptop or tablet where people can opt into your mailing list on the spot. These email addresses come in handy when you thank every person a day later for coming to your book launch.

In addition, don't forget those who helped you in any way. You will want to write to those who did not make it. Kindly tell them they were missed and where your book can be purchased – whether online or in a store. Post your photos and video immediately after the event. Add more images over the period of a week or so, in order to spread out the fun and reminders.

Enjoy meeting the people who are interested in your book! Have fun at the party! Writing and author-publishing a book is a great accomplishment – a reason to celebrate.

There Are Dozens of Online Book Retailers

There are more online retailers for e-books and books than just Amazon, Apple, Kobo or Barnes & Noble, not to mention the numerous online book retailers in the UK and in other parts of the world.

Here are just a few more online book retailers where you can sell your book in North America, Europe and elsewhere:

- *www.Scribd.com*
- *www.booksonboard.com/*
- *www.ebooks.com*
- *www.ebook-store-review.toptenreviews.com*
- *www.ebookmall.com*
- *www.indiebound.org*
- *www.24symbols.com/*
- *www.powells.com/ebooks/*
- *www.kobobooks.com/eBooks*
- *www.rbooks.co.uk/ebook.aspx* UK

- www.whsmith.co.uk/eBooks.aspx UK
- www.waterstones.com/waterstonesweb/browse/ebooks/4294964587/ UK
- *Thalia* Germany
  http://www.thalia.de/shop/home/show/
- *Thalia* Austria
  http://www.thalia.at/shop/home/show/
- *Thalia* Switzerland
  http://www.thalia.ch/shop/home/show/
- *Weltbild* Germany
  https://www.weltbild.de/
- *Weltbild* Austria
  https://www.weltbild.at/
- *Weltbild* Switzerland
  https://www.weltbild.ch/
- *Buecher* Germany
  http://www.buecher.de/
- *Buch* Germany
  http://www.buch.de/shop/home/show/
- *Hugendubel* Germany
  http://www.hugendubel.de/de/
- *eBook* Germany
  http://www.ebook.de/
- *Bol* Germany
  http://www.bol.de/shop/home/show/

- *Mayersche* Germany
  http://www.mayersche.de/

- *Osiander* Germany
  https://www.osiander.de/

- *Libris* Netherlands
  http://libris.nl/

- *Osiander* Germany
  https://www.osiander.de/

- *Books* Switzerland
  http://www.books.ch/shop/home/show/

- *Buch* Switzerland
  https://www.orellfuessli.ch/shop/home/show/

- *Mandadori* Italy
  http://www.mondadori.com/our-brands/books

- *Angus & Robertson* Australia
  https://www.angusrobertson.com.au/

Don't Put All Your Eggs in One Basket

You don't have to upload to all these booksellers or deal with their payment process by yourself. Sell your books through distributors worldwide. A former article: *Who is the best?* provides a book distributor comparison lists of most of the reliable distributors (also called aggregators) in North America and Europe. *Draft2Digital* – https://www.draft2digital.com/ – is in my experience – as a publisher for several authors – one of the best distributors.

Another reason to use a distributor: If you are you living outside the USA as an independent author and you don't want to go through all the hassle with opening a US branch for your publishing business. Barnes & Noble, for example, doesn't deal with foreign authors, and they also require US-Bank accounts from their suppliers in order to pay out revenue for books sold.

If you don't want to upload your book yourself, get help from this aggregator for one small yearly fee and reap 100% of your retailer's revenue: *eBookPartnership.com* – *http://ebookpartnership.com/*. They have a global reach and a flat fee with 0% Commission. Their online distribution service reaches more than 150 e-book retailers and offers to 65,000+ libraries. Aggregators will handle distribution, sales, and accepting payments. They manage your account with online retailers.

Indiebound.org

Indiebound – http://indiebound.org/ – offers more than 3.5 million titles. Check out the independent bookstores in your city or state that are participating at Indibound.org and upload your book or e-book to Kobo. Arrange a book signing with these "brick & mortar stores".

Indiebound.org's website also offers a map of North America, which is the "Indie Store Finder" for the USA and Canada. This feature has lists of all the indie bookstores in your area.

What to Prepare Before Uploading to Retailers/Distributors:

Before uploading your print or ebook use this *list – http://www.savvybookwriters.com/what-to-prepare-before-uploading-to-retailersdistributors/ –* to make sure you have all the information needed at hand:

- ePub file (mobi for Amazon) of your book (for eBooks) (pdf for your print books) printed works and e-books need to be uploaded separately!

- Cover image in jpeg format – Ideal dimensions for cover files are 2,560 x 1,600 pixels – at Amazon at least. Somewhere else 2400x1600 pixels are recommended. Find out your distributor's size requirements.

- Title and subtitle – if there are no two fields, place it in one

- Edition: only fill it out if it is not the first edition, but a second or third

- Author name (or pen name)

- Book Description: The book description goes on the back cover (for paperbacks) or the inside flap copy (for hard copies) and right below the price (online retailers). It's crucial that this short paragraph is catching the interest of readers and packed with keywords. Don't write it like a summery, rather like an ad. Most important is the first, catchy line.

- About the author: Everything related to your writing career.

- 7 – 10 Keywords / Meta tags (the most important first) – readers need to find your book

- ISBN (buy your own!)

- BISAC code # (to choose the genres under which bookstores and libraries shelf your book). *Find the complete BISAC book categories here – https://bisg.org/page/bisacedition*

- "Determine the major heading which best describes the content of your book. Click on one of the headings listed on the Complete BISAC Subject Heading page for more specific headings within that category.

- Once you've selected a major category (for example, Fiction), determine the specific term which describes your book. You may select more than one subject code, but no more than three BISAC codes," explains the organization.

- Amazon's genres are slightly different from those. So it's a good idea to first check out your Amazon "competition" to see in which categories they placed their book. Find the categories that best match your books based on your content. Study carefully each book that is competitive to yours and see in which categories the bestsellers among them are listed. Narrow down your list as much as possible. You can also email Amazon's KDP and ask them to get your book into the proper categories, telling them the exact line. Here is an example of what a difference in competing books it makes when choosing the right genre

- Decide at which retailers you want to sell your book – and in which countries. For example, you can choose among these retailers: Barnes & Noble, Kobo, iBooks, Scribd, Playster, Inktera, 24Symbols, H.S.Smith, Tolino Books (goes to Weltbild, Thalia, Hugendubel etc. in German-speaking countries) and OverDrive (delivers to Libraries).

- Set the price for each country – considering their country-specific sales tax

Sell From Your Own Website

If you want to keep (almost) all revenue from your books, then sell from your own website! It is so easy these days to implement a "turn-key" e-commerce page on your web presence. The greatest benefit for you as the author is that you get the data of your buyers! You will know who reads your books or gives it as a present. Data you would never receive from Amazon or other retailers!

There are several IT companies who are running the sales and payment process for a small fee for you – no matter if e-books, audiobooks or the print version. Just to mention a few of the many e-stores available:

Shopify – https://www.shopify.ca/

EJunkie – https://www.e-junkie.com/

Ganxy – http://get.ganxy.com/

Selz – https://selz.com/ or

Gumroad – https://gumroad.com/.

With a Little Help from Your Friends…

No matter if you are an author with lots of friends, or if you are the friend of an author, the bestseller list will help you to find out how Amazon's algorithm determines the popularity of books and their visibility (which is different from the sales rank). The bestseller list and the popularity list are two very different things. How this list is determined is dependent on Amazon's current algorithms. For instance, free downloads carry far less weight now than they did in the past. These little features take only a few seconds but can make a difference in the popularity list. Ask your friends to do the following:

Write Reviews

Write reviews, especially on Amazon and Goodreads, even if the book you read, already has lots of reviews. The more reviews the better for the author. This also means that more potential buyers can see the popularity of the work. Make a copy of your review and send it to all the other online booksellers as well! Before you can post a review, you are required to have an Amazon account that you have used for a purchase in the value of $50.

Highlights

Here is another item in Amazon's algorithm list for book popularity: If you have a Kindle, you can highlight some wise or fun quotations from the book and share them publicly. If enough people share their highlights, the will show up in your e-book.

Amazon displays "Popular Highlights" by combining the highlights of all Kindle customers and identifying the passages with the most highlights. The resulting popular highlights help readers focus on passages that are meaningful to the greatest number of people. Popular highlights are marked with a grey dashed underline. The number of people who have highlighted the text appears at the beginning of the marked text.

Reviews, Tags, or Highlights, it all helps to boost the books' rankings in Amazon's popularity list (not the bestseller list!). Take two books with identical sales numbers: the one which has been promoted with these features will be higher on the list. It will definitely have more visibility and sell better in the future.

Amazon's Algorithm

In the past, book sales that went through the roof on their first day of sale on Amazon got high rankings. Right now, Amazon's algorithms prefer "steady" sales. So, there is no more need to push all your friends to buy your new book on a certain day. And also no need to pin the perception of your book's success on a single day of sales – and no adrenaline rush of having instant success! You can stay focused on a much more sustainable metric: average sales per day or week.

Get More Book Reviews

Reviews sell books. The more you have, the more credibility you will have with your potential buyers. Reader/writer forums and social media seem to be the best places to solicit book reviews. Why, you might ask? Well, as a member you are known and appreciated; you have "personal" contact with these folks. For that reason, they are more inclined to do something for you, the writer. Join communities at Wattpad, Google+, Shelfari, RedRoom, Goodreads, LibraryThing, KindleBoards and so forth. Networking on these sites is the only option to make a name for a self-publishing writer.

You may also want to contact magazines and newspapers who regularly review books. Find out on Amazon and Goodreads who are the "top reviewers" and see if you can befriend them on social media. In our book on *111 Tips to Get FREE Book Reviews – http://www.apple.com/: Best Strategies for Getting Lots of Great Reviews"* we go into all the details, and you will find more than 1,200 direct links to book bloggers and reviewers. In addition we regularly give tips where to find reviewers in our monthly newsletters.

Cross Promotions and Blog Tours

It's important to join reader and writer communities, online and in "real life". They are an important part of your discoverability. They will help to spread the word about you as a writer and about your books. Think guest blogs, blog tours, and author interviews:

Blog Tours

A blog tour is a kind of press tour in the blogging sphere. A writer creates a guest blog for a well-known book blogging site. Usually, the guest blog also involves a book giveaway. Blog tours can last from one week to one month and usually involve a dozen different blogs. Writers use the bloggers to promote the books. Bloggers use the writers' names and a giveaway to promote their website. Bloggers often ask for giveaways: free items that they will give to one lucky commenter or reader. The giveaway could be a copy of the book you are promoting or an advance copy.

Blog Interviews

Sometimes a blog tour includes interviews. It works like this: the blogger sends you a series of questions by e-mail, and then you respond by e-mail. Those questions can run for pages or only five or six lines. Authors can certainly trade interviews with their writing/blogging friends.

Create a Slide Show for Your Book

Think PowerPoint presentation. *SlideShare* – *http://www.slideshare.net/* – is a site where you can host your presentations and share them with others. Slideshows can be linked to the site itself or embedded in your webpage. SlideShare is a popular and FREE service that allows anyone to upload a presentation onto the site, then send a URL to enable anyone to view the document. These presentations are static, comparable to PowerPoint presentations. File sharing services have been around for decades. However, SlideShare was one of the first ones to successfully allow people to view, share and socialize an entire presentation directly onto a Web page without any downloading.

The Power of Book Trailers

You might have read my book *111 Tips to Create Your Book Trailer – http://www.amazon.com/dp/B008Y15YYO* – in which I explained that book trailers are one of the best ways to introduce your book to millions of readers worldwide. Readers of *111 Tips to Create Your Book Trailer – http://www.amazon.com/dp/B008Y15YYO* – will explore:

- which audience their trailer will attract for the book's genre
- how to find design ideas for a book trailer
- how to set the mood for their book
- which music fits the style of your book
- what video software is available
- where to publicize the book trailer for free

Learn how to plan and create your video in *111 Tips to Create Impressive Videos – https://www.books2read.com/u/3GYnpa*. The most important step, marketing your video, is also explained step by step in this valuable guidebook. Check also out tips for free music, free graphics and images, and free video hosting sites on our *blog – http://savvybookwriters.com/blog*. Just type in your search words and the articles will appear. Also, don't forget to post your video(s) on your Amazon, Goodreads, Google+, and other social media sites.

The possibility that internet users will click on a short video or slideshow is much, much higher than the possibility that they will read a text description. They will also be more likely to send a link to your book trailer to their friends, or to a social media site – more likely than to share a text description of your book. A recent survey found that video content in web pages or emails increased click-through rates by 96%!

Video engages your audience more than text because it includes sights and sounds. Thanks to upload-sites and popular video sharing sites, such as *Instagram – https://help.instagram.com/442610612501386*, iTunes, YouTube.com, Google Video and Yahoo (which have millions of views per day), publishers and writers can post their book trailers for the whole world to see. The key is to create a video that people want to pass on to their friends and connections. Read more about how to plan, create, upload and market your video creation in *111 Tips to Create Impressive Videos – https://www.books2read.com/u/3GYnpa*.

PART FIVE

In this chapter, you will learn about advanced marketing strategies and how you can leverage your manuscript in markets other than e-book or paperback. Again: there is lots of information in this guide to book marketing and professional publishing. My advice is to read it chapter by chapter, paragraph by paragraph. Otherwise, you might be overwhelmed by too much information. I want to inform and make suggestions – not overload you.

Book Marketing Strategies

Selling your book for a very low price, or for free, is only a viable marketing strategy under these conditions:

- You already have a name as an author
- You have several books under your belt
- You are a well-established author

It should only be done, and only works well, in these circumstances. It costs money to advertise for free days, and then you lose sales. Free days will soon be over. Following the sale of a couple of books, your book will revert back to its old Amazon rankings. Consider this, too: you must commit to exclusivity with Amazon for 90 days. It means that you must remove your e-book (NOT the print version!) from all other retailers. You must give up your e-book royalties from Barnes & Noble, Kobo, Apple iBook store or wherever else you sell it.

A Much Better Incentive for Readers:

To give away a short story (1000 to 1,500 words), or to write a guest blog post, or a newspaper or magazine article is a much better approach to get attention – and you can include a link to your book's sales page. Publishing stories with a high-traffic magazine, newspaper, or websites will help you to find new readers and you might get even paid for it. You can split your book into many short stories. Re-write or spin it a bit to make it "like new". If you tweet or post about these free short stories, your book will receive an additional promotion.

Your article will also link to your sales page and your own website. On your site, you hopefully have an opt-in form for your email newsletter to invite readers to your next book's launch. Here's another benefit of short stories: You can test the popularity of future books. If you want to sell your writing, you need to know what your readers want. "Test the waters" before you start writing your next book.

The Most Successful KDP Free Day Campaigns

Authors with multiple books, or a series of books, use promotion days to give away the first book in a series. They hope that customers will come back and buy the other books from these series, which they often do. You can use each of your books to advertise everything else you have written. Don't forget: If you have only one book, there is nothing that readers can actually buy from you after they have received your book for free!

Alternative: Pay-With-a-Tweet Campaign

Another, and more sustainable method is to give away your book for free – after the recipient has tweeted (or posted) about your book. It's called "Pay-with-a-Tweet", and the benefits are: you don't need to lock your book exclusively to Amazon Select, you can sell your e-book at the same time on Barnes & Noble, Kobo, Chapters etc.. Every free download creates buzz. You don't have to sign up or pay for advertising your free book – and it has a good chance to go viral. The fact that you, not Amazon, choose how often (and when) you can campaign is another benefit. You will also learn about your readers.

Selling Books and e-Books to Libraries

U.S. Libraries purchase books for nearly $2 billion per year. Not only books but also audiobooks and e-books. Most libraries acquire only brand new books. Once you have written several bestselling books, you can think about selling your latest one to libraries. Imagine: if you sold your $15 book at a 50% discount to only 5% of the 100,000 libraries in the USA. You would earn more than $37,000. But how can you reach out to this lucrative market? What are the distribution channels?

Quality Books Inc. – *http://www.quality-books.com/* – provides libraries with small press books that are not widely available through other distributors. Their inventory is devoted ONLY to libraries. They explain: "Our Title Selection Committee is made up of two MLS-degreed librarians and three publishing professionals. The committee uses more than 20 criteria with which to evaluate every title submitted to QBI for possible distribution." They give detailed information on what they are looking for on Quality Book's webpage. They also state clearly how to submit your book, audiobook, CD etc.

Another major distributor to libraries is *UniqueBooksInc – http://www.uniquebooksinc.com/*. This company specializes in non-fiction books and DVDs. Their website states: "We are a full- service library resource – providing our customers with newly copyrighted titles. Unique Books Inc. solves the small press dilemma of reaching the elusive, high maintenance library market profitably."

OverDrive – https://www.overdrive.com/, owned by Rakuten-Kobo, is the main distributor to libraries and has more than 1,000,000 e-book titles available and growing. They were the early pioneers in the digital lending space. They developed the e-book lending systems used by most libraries today. Overdrive uses the same Adobe DRM (Digital Rights Management) system as Kobo, Barnes & Noble, and Google Books to protect files from piracy and manage the lending period of library e-books. Overdrive also offers a program called "Advantage" where individual libraries and library systems buy extra titles or copies to fill a local demand. Read more details in my article *Myths And Truth About Selling to Libraries – http://savvybookwriters.wordpress.com/2013/11/19/myths-and-truth-about-selling-to-libraries*.

Read from Your Books at Libraries

Many libraries offer "Author Talks and Lectures" for adults, teens, and children. It is relatively easy to get an appointment with your local library organizer. Plan well ahead (three to six months); they have to include the event in their brochures and on their websites. You can offer readings, tell stories, or talk about the writing and publishing process. You can also offer them a whole series of talks about researching, writing, and the book marketing process. Many people in your audience might order your book. Bring your laptop or tablet, so they can order it right away if they want. Don't forget to bring bookmarks, or business cards, so the attendees can hand them out to their friends or family.

How to Get Your Print Books into Airport Bookstores

Airport bookstores get lots of traffic and exposure. Sales are what concerns these stores and the reason why they are careful about what they shelve. Books at travel hubs, such as airports and train stations, generally have to have:

- a fabulous and enticing book cover layout
- a kind of book that appeals to travelers
- a compelling price to prompt impulse purchases
- an ISBN, EAN barcode and its price printed on the rear cover

Which Books Sell Best to Travelers?

Beside novels – mystery or romance – and non-fiction themes, such as computers, cars, food, health, finance, fitness, and even children's books (as a gift or for their little family members during the flight) is what interests many travelers. During the holiday season and the long summertime is when airport book purchases thrive.

Even if your first, self-published work is amazing and sports an enticing cover: you might have to offer more titles, great sales numbers and lots of positive reviews from professional media outlets – preferably a "#1 Bestseller" sticker.

However, even if you possess all these, there is no guarantee that the airport bookstores will carry your titles. After all, books from Agatha Christie, Danielle Steel, Alexandre Dumas, Charles Dickens, Nora Roberts, Jane Austen, Jackie Collins, James Patterson, Victor Hugo, Jules Verne, J. K. Rowling, Jack Higgins, Stephen King, and Leon Uris are your competition in these stores.

Find out if the distributor of your books delivers to airport bookstores, and contact them to learn what you can do to with this endeavour. It might be a good idea to get a second or third distributor for your books who have contracts with WH Smith in the UK – eBookPartnership for example and even Baker & Taylor, IngramSpark or ReaderLink – which are distributing to some airport stores. Publishers and Indies can contact purchasers of airport bookstores directly, such as:

- W.H. Smith and *WHSmith Booksellers* – *https://www.whsmith.co.uk/* – operates or owns 255 airport shops and 421 hotel stores in the UK and Europe

- *HMSHost Corporation – https://www.hmshost.com/about/interior/airports*, which operates fourteen "Simply Books" bookstores in airports right now, mainly in Southern states.

- Download a Consignment Program information from *Booksinc – https://www.booksinc.net/411#authors* – airport locations in California

- *ReaderLink – http://www.readerlink.net/* – is the largest full-service distributor of hardcover, trade and paperback books to 24,000 non-trade channel booksellers in North America

- *Paradies-Lagardere – http://paradieslagardere.com/contact-us/business-inquiries/*, with headquarters in Atlanta and Toronto, cater to airport travelers in all of North America, and even the Caribbean.

Offer Your Book to Book Discussion Clubs

They are more often called simply a book club, reading group, book group, or book discussion group. A book (discussion) club is a group of people who meet to discuss a book that they have all read. They express their opinions, likes, and dislikes. Book discussion clubs meet in private homes, libraries, bookstores, online forums, pubs, and in cafes or restaurants. Typically, books will get chosen by the group through the input of all members.

It might be worth it to find out the contact information of book clubs via Google search in your city, county, province or state. You can offer them your book for discussion. If you become a member of a book discussion group, you might have even more luck.

How to Profit from an Award

Winning a book award for your self-published fiction or nonfiction book is a great way to gain recognition and approval. Publicity around a book award will boost your book sales. Most awards call for entries every year. If the competition is closed for this year, mark your calendar for next year's contest call. There are hundreds of options that range from scams to high-level, great exposure. Before you click on "accept" when applying, or pay any money, carefully read the small print in order to avoid giving your rights away for free. Google the award's name; you might be surprised sometimes.

Here are a few of the most popular book contests:

- *http://www.narrativemagazine.com/node/249923*
- *http://www.independentpublisher.com/ipland/ipawards.php*
- *http://www.usabooknews.com/2014usabestbookawards.html*
- *http://www.cbc.ca/books/canadawrites/literaryprizes/nonfiction/*
- *http://www.writersdigest.com/competitions/selfpub-lished*
- *http://ibpabenjaminfranklinawards.com/*

- *http://readersfavorite.com/annual-book-award-contest.htm*
- *http://www.cbc.ca/books/canadawrites/literaryprizes/shortstory/index.html*
- *http://www.pw.org/grants*

How Will You Market Your Award?

If you have written or published an "award-winning book" selected from hundreds of competing titles (by an experienced, professional team of judges), it will have been given a seal of excellence. It's good to win the award. Publicize the fact that your book has been chosen among hundreds of others is equally important. Add "award-winning" to your e-mail signature. Post a press release and write a blog post about it. Create a guest post about your experience including tips for other writers. Do as many book signings as possible accompanied by a huge poster of your award. Offer your work to book clubs, mentioning your award.

Get Interviews on Radio and TV Shows

Your book sales will certainly not skyrocket after a radio show like *The Book Report* – *http://www.bookreportradio.com/*, but it will be archived on YouTube and iTunes. You can also make subtle posts and tweets about your book and your radio appearance. After you are interviewed by a local radio station, please keep this in mind: traditional media endorsements, even if it's simply mentioning your name, are "marketing gold".

Such publicity gets your book into more readers' hands. Don't miss the opportunity to let everyone know about it. You can post it on YouTube and all the free video sharing sites and certainly on all your author pages at online retailers.

The Book Report – *http://www.bookreportradio.com/schedule.html* – with Host Elaine Charles is a fun, fast-moving, fact-filled show in 10 major markets across the USA. Check out their radio stations and show schedules. They have a lively mix of author interviews, audiobook previews, and chats with those influential in the literary world. Bibliophiles and book clubs alike make appointments to listen to *The Book Report*. It's a great way to find out who's hot in the book world and which titles critics and readers are buzzing about.

For non-fiction writers: check out *these tips* – *http://copalche.rssing.com/chan-1135339/all_p1.html* – on how to get a guest spot as an expert on a radio talk show and what presenters are looking for. There are also lots of tips on how to get a (small) chance to be featured on a TV talk show at *ScriptMag* – *http://www.scriptmag.com/features/primetime-how-can-i-be-a-guest-expert-on-talk-or-reality-shows*.

Improve Visibility for Your Books

Online book sites, such as Barnes & Noble (which offers several slots with books in the same genre), Amazon, and Apple have all listing at the bottom of your book's sales page screen that says "Customers also bought" or "People who bought this book also bought …" It shows all the books of your competition – if you have only one or two books listed with them. Their "Customers also bought" lists can be found on print sites or e-book sites (or both). So, what can you do as an author to avoid having similar books recommended on your sales page?

Write More Books

If you write more books (say between three and nine books), and readers like what you do, guess whose books appear in the listings mentioned above? Yours! If you only publish one book, then those slots get filled with books written by other authors. These book suggestions show that readers who liked your book also bought these other books. A great example of a prolific writer with more than 20 books is Jan Scarbrough. Just click on one of her books, scroll down, and you will see lots of her other books shown under "Customers Who Bought This Item Also Bought…"

Start Maximizing Your Foreign Presence – For FREE

To maximize your presence in overseas Amazon Kindle stores, just set up an Author Central account in each of the country-specific sites where your book is available. Announce your Countdown Deals, new book launches, or Free Kindle KDP Days in several languages because Amazon divided the world into single countries: Order a short translation of 10 tweets in Spanish, French, German, and more for $5 per 200 words at *fiverr.com* – http://www.fiverr.com/, or use the services at *elance.com* – http://www.elance.com/. The countries with the most usage of e-Readers, according to a BookBoon survey, are the USA, UK, Netherlands, Belgium, France, Germany, Austria, Switzerland, and Denmark.

Write More Short Stories

It might take years until you have written so many books that only your books show up as suggestions. An even better way to promote your writing is to write and sell short stories as e-books (either self-published or traditionally). Unlike book publishers, short story publishers only hold on to exclusive rights to the story for a limited period of time. After that period of time, either the rights revert to you or they become non-exclusive.

Read more about book contracts and rights in my former blog posts at SavvyBookWriters. Your copyright license lasts for a certain period of time. After this period of time – specified by your publishing contract – you can then put your short story up as an e-book or put it in an e-book collection of your own (or both). You won't have to remove that story from the first place of publication. If you self-publish your short stories, you can do whatever you want! You don't need to wait until your publishing contract expires. Short story markets will allow new readers to sample your work.

Sampling is the Best Way to Hook a Reader!

Retail businesses know the importance of sampling. It works in grocery stores. I almost always buy food novelties after I can try them. Then, there are the many samples shown in the weekly flyers. Personal products, such as shampoo or body lotions, get promoted through hotels to their guests. In the past, some publishers would offer the first chapter of each book in their new book listings. However, they only handed these reading samples out at book fairs or to bookstore owners. Hardly anyone reads them. Now, readers can download samples of any book published electronically. If readers like the book, they will most likely buy it.

Write a FREE e-Book

It doesn't need to be a full-length novel, just more than a short story. You certainly can incorporate your other book's sales page links, your social media links, and even ready-to-click tweets about your book. Readers want to know more and interact with the author whose book they are buying. They don't want to see only ads with the message: "Buy my book! Buy my book! Buy my Book!" Rather, readers want to see samples of your writing before they purchase more of your books.

Connect All Your Social Networking Sites

Start with your blog. The time you spend posting can be massively shortened through scheduling. It can also be shortened by connecting your blog with your social media sites and connecting them with each other, using plug-ins. For instance, you can set up your social media presence on Google+, Twitter, LinkedIn, Goodreads, Facebook, Tumblr, and StumpleUpon to join with each other. Post something on Google+, and it will automatically be a tweet. Schedule a tweet, and it will automatically go to several other social media sites. Your blog can appear on Goodreads. You can write up to 500 characters in each post on Google+ – more than on any other social media site.

LinkedIn, Pinterest, and Bit.ly can be set up with one click to have every message or post automatically sent to

Twitter – at least the first 140 characters. Free scheduling services, such as *Hootsuite – http://www.hootsuite.com/ –*, *FutureTweets – http://.futuretweets.com/ –* and *Tweetadder – http://tweetadder.com/ –*, can be set up to ping your posts automatically to Twitter and Facebook. They certainly offer their paid scheduling, but there is not much difference, and it's not really worth using their paid version, unless you are keen on their statistic features. *This article – http://savvybookwriters.wordpress.com/2012/12/18/how-to-automatically-post-on-twitter-from-your-google-page* – explains how to automatically post on Twitter from your Google+ page and *this article – http://savvybookwriters.wordpress.com/2014/07/07/5-google-tips-for-advanced-users* – explains how to connect Google+ with YouTube.

Book Signings at Local Bookstores

Start with your own local bookstores. Some will agree to a book signing with a local author. However, just because you set up an event doesn't mean people will come! You have to announce it to as many people as possible. In the weeks leading up to the book signing, promote it often on all your social media sites, and on Craigslist or other local websites.

Print out some flyers and post them at libraries, on community boards, in coffee shops etc. Perhaps a local radio station will announce it. Send out a press release to various local media outlets; offer them a free digital version of your book. Don't forget to mention in your invitations that you will have a drawing or sweepstake (maybe for a Kindle eReader or a small tablet). You should also announce that you will have "refreshments" (coffee and cookies, or even wine and cheese).

It all depends on the venue. In a chain bookstore that includes a coffee shop, you may want to consider handing out a gift card for a large coffee to people who bought your book. Bring your bookmarks or cards, a fishbowl to collect addresses for the drawing to win another book of yours, lots of pens, and water for yourself.

Get Your Book Translated Into World Languages

You can certainly translate your book and sell it through online retailers worldwide. Why translating your own manuscripts? In one sentence: More money, more books to offer, a completely new readership, you double your success. Even if you are not self-publishing, and going with a trade publisher, it's possible to have your book(s) in other languages – provided you have retained your publishing rights in other languages than English. Repurpose the hard work you put into writing the English book – in all formats, such as the digital version, a print book, or audiobook version.

According to Wikipedia, the most widely spoken languages besides English (although this doesn't necessarily relate to e-book readers) are Mandarin, Spanish, Hindi, Arabic, German, Russian, Portuguese, Bengali, and Japanese.

The German language and Germany should be the first choice for self-publishing in translation due to the growing e-reader base on Amazon.de and the Tolino-Thalia-Weltbild connection.

If funds are not an issue, hire a professional and recommended translator for your book. Here is a *complete list of translator and interpreter associations – https://en.wikipedia.org/wiki/List_of_translators_and_interpreters_associations*:

The second (inexpensive) method would be to let Google Translation or BabelCube do the job and then hire a native speaker (teacher or other languages professional) to edit the translation. Another option is to band with a translator and exercise the "royalty split translation model" – a royalty split model for translation.

Your translation is free, but your translator will get a certain percentage of your book sales. The royalty split can be better financially in the long run and you get a marketing partner in the language of translation. This means that you get your emails for review pitches, blog interviews etc. translated.

All the ongoing work of building the book in the market is shared between the author and the translator. You can trust the work of the translator more as they won't get paid unless the book is good enough to sell. They have a vested interest in making the work the best it can be. The risk is split between you and there is no upfront payment, so it's easy to try things out. It certainly needs a written contract – but everything else only works when there is trust on both sides.

You can also use *BabelCube* – https://www.babelcube.com/ – for any of the 15+ languages and royalty split deals. They offer a distribution platform and take 15% royalty and their translator/rights holder split varies on the number of books sold. There are no upfront costs – just share the royalties! Choose your translator – or a team of them. Authors will be able to sell their book in world languages through hundreds of online retail channels and subscription services. Read more about this and other translation platforms in our *blog article* – *http://www.savvybookwriters.com/how-to-sell-translated-german-language-books-overseas/*.

Sell Your Foreign Rights

Foreign rights can be a great way to leverage the value of your manuscript, but don't expect big numbers right away. Revenue will be paid as an advance: approximately 6% – 10% royalty of the retail price, minus the percentage for the agent. This is also a long-term project. It takes around eighteen months until the book is translated and finally available online and in bookstores.

Foreign rights are part of your book's subsidiary rights. Like other sub-rights (such as audio, movie, book club, paperback reprint, and electronic rights), foreign rights can be sold and separated from your book's primary rights. You own these rights anyway as an independent author-publisher. Always contact your national writers' association for further information, and get legal advice from a lawyer who specializes in copyrights, before you sign a contract. This could save you several thousand dollars – if not more.

How About a Movie Deal for Your Book?

Book adaptations into a movie have become one of the fastest growing, most reliably profitable and attractive markets for producers in Hollywood, such as *Harry Potter* or the Canadian author Margaret Atwood's *The Handmaid's Tale*.

There are several directions one can follow – or all of them at the same time:

1. Literary Agents or Publishers
2. Film Agents
3. Film Producers

Movie rights are part of sub rights (or subsidiary rights). Even so, these rights are hard to sell. If you get a foot in the door, almost all production companies and film producers offer an option for a film first. What exactly is an option?

Fred Rosen – http://www.writersstore.com/authors/fred-rosen – explains what options are: "It is a rental. A production company or studio reserves the right to make your work into a film, MOW or TV show for a specific length of time. In the past, the standard option was for a year, with two renewable one-year options. Taking advantage of the recent recession, producers have now been able to negotiate the first option to 18 months.

Regardless, each time a company picks up the option, you get paid just for sitting on your movie rights. In the meantime, they'll try to secure the money to make the adaptation and get someone to write the script (though it probably won't be you – Hollywood prefers to use its own writers to adapt work)." He further explains what can get optioned:

"Just about anything can get optioned. Published novels and non-fiction books. Magazine articles. Short stories. Unpublished work can break through, too, when someone who has a connection with a production company discovers something and passes it on (Frank Capra based *It's a Wonderful Life* on an unpublished short story by Philip Van Doren Stern). But you should generally focus on getting published first – because the print imprimatur still demands the highest price when optioned."

How Much is an Option Worth?

Fred Rosen says: "Options start at $500 and go up. In today's market, $5,000 and more is excellent. It's impossible to offer an average because it depends on so many factors, the most important being how much the production company wants the work."

Do I Need a Film Agent to Make the Option Sale?

Rosen says: "Generally, yes. If you have a literary agent, look at your contract and see if the agent gets points for a film sale. If so, encourage her to send your work to a film agent she's familiar with (the two will split the commission). If you don't have an agent, it's fine to query film agents directly. They're always looking for salable stuff to pitch to Hollywood.

Be straightforward in your pitch: Briefly summarize the work to be optioned, where it's published and your bio." Read all of *Fred Rosen's tips* – *http://www.writersdigest.com/whats-new/selling-your-books-movie-and-tv-rights-what-you-need-to-know* here and get an idea how much you might earn. Important also is to read this article by Kristine Kathrin Rusch *Stealing Intellectual Property – http://kriswrites. com/tag/intellectual-property/* before you do anything. She explains in detail how authors can be tricked into unfavorable movie contracts.

Be VERY Patient. Making a movie can take up to 5-10 years or more. If you're not willing or able to invest that kind of time, why would a producer want to help you out? BE PERSISTENT! Don't stop to send out queries. Know that it is not easy to get a movie deal.

How Else Can You Leverage Your Manuscript?

You can sell parts of your book to:

- one publisher
- other parts to another publisher
- some parts to overseas markets
- other parts to audio
- others as e-Books or Singles
- to game companies
- maybe to Hollywood's film industry

You can also submit parts of it to contests, or divide it into chapters and sell it to magazines or a web publisher. The list of possibilities goes on and on. This is what you need to do:

- Learn all about copyright in order to really understand it

- Realize that each piece can be a cash stream for you

- Choose a name. (You don't even have to use your name.) You can choose a pen name or even several

You can sell these rights or uses them in several ways:
First Serial Rights

These can be print or electronic. It means that you are selling a publisher the right to be the first to publish your article for one time only. In the case of print rights, you may immediately sell the piece to an e-publisher, even before print publication. After the print magazine, containing your article, hits the newsstand, you are free to sell it again as a reprint to other print markets.

First Serial Rights (Electronic)

Most Canadian and US freelance authors sell North American first serial rights, reserving the right to sell in other world markets (e.g. Great Britain, Australia or Asia). Specify what type of rights you are selling: first North American electronic rights only.

Second Serial Rights

These are reprint rights that apply to both the print and electronic markets. Never sell reprint rights – keep them at all costs. Even though you will earn less money for each reprint, you are able sell your work over and over again.

Subsidiary Rights

Other rights that authors and freelancers hold are subsidiary rights, including, but not limited to the following: movie rights, TV and radio rights, audio and other media rights.

Each story, each novel is a piece of your writing business. If you spread them out over a number of pen names, you will have a pretty consistent cash flow going. You just need to offer them to people who will buy them. For instance: you sold your German translation rights, and your contract with the German publisher limited your book to trade paper only. Now you can sell the following:

- German hardback rights
- German audio rights
- German mass market rights
- German film rights

Your German publisher will pay advances in the same manner as your Canadian or American publisher. In addition, there will be royalties (against advances). At that point, maybe you can sell your work to Spanish, Russian, or Italian publishing houses. Dozens and dozens of pieces of your work can be sold. Each piece contributes to the cash stream. You just need to sell it. You create the inventory (your book) just once. But you can sell it for your entire life. Wring maximum value out of your book by spinning off audios, videos, magazine excerpts, foreign-language editions, and more. Multipurpose your book into other forms: downloadable

CD's and e-book versions, audiotapes, videotapes, magazine excerpts, and foreign language editions are a few of the options.

Kindle Singles

You might have written articles and submitted them to e-zines or "content farms" for free. You would have added your web links hoping that readers would click on these links and come to your website to buy books – or whatever you offer there.

Now, it is possible to write anywhere from 5,000- to 30,000- word articles. Amazon calls them "Kindle Singles" and sells them online. A prominent author of these Kindle Singles is Stephen King, who wrote "Mile 81". It's the current top seller – as of this writing. Therefore, instead of submitting your work for free to content farms, you can sell those articles at the website of the internet giant, Amazon. You will receive 70% royalties, even for Singles priced under $2.99. To be precise you will receive them for Singles priced between $0.99 and $4.99.

Other criteria for Amazon Singles include:

- original work; not previously published in other formats or publications

- self-contained work; not chapters excerpted from a longer work

- not published on any public website in its entirety

Amazon is not currently accepting how-to manuals, public domain works, reference books, travel guides, or children's books!

Split Your Book Into Single Articles

Very few emerging writers realize that they can sell their magazine articles over and over again. As long as the markets don't overlap, you can sell exactly the same article as many times as you like. In addition, in this globally connected marketplace, it is easier than you think.

However, you can only sell first rights, either print or electronic, once for the same piece. After that, unless you change the article significantly, you must offer it as a reprint for a lower fee. If you change the article, you can sell it again for first rights. For example, you can turn a 500-word piece for a grade seven market into an article of similar length for a regional Catholic newspaper and an Anglican website (e-rights) in Canada.

You can even tweak it into an 800-word article for a national U.S. daily. Subsequently, you can make some minor changes to slant the piece for a travel magazine. Each time, you will be able to sell it for first rights. Continue to sell it. However, be on the lookout for new markets in other English language markets overseas.

This practice should be your the standard operating procedure if you write and sell articles to print or online periodicals. It makes good business and time management sense to resell your work. It reduces the energy you expend and increases your revenue. Unless you routinely sell a single article for several thousands of dollars (perhaps even if you do), you should be squeezing every dollar out of every single piece you write.

Bestseller Tips – From Trade Publishers

How can author-publishers use the methods of global trade publishers to promote their self-published books? You don't need to travel to the Frankfurt Book Fair in Germany like Johannes Kepler did in 1620. Yes, self-publishing was en vogue already four-hundred years ago!

You can also use some traditional marketing methods to create a business plan. Traditional publishing uses multiple ways to promote. It seems that self-published authors attempt to market their books to the entire world via Amazon, social media, and their website. Publishers select books in order to stay in business, and also to determine what the publishing house's identity is. Here's how you can copy traditional ways to market--adjusted to self-publishing: one step at a time, but continually every day; split these into small tasks.

Start Early

Market Research is the very first step! An editor will need to make a case that the book fills a market need. In order to do that, the publishing house will look carefully at what's out there. Does the competition have a recent publication in this sub-genre? Does it have a similar scope? Is it widely available?

Authors, especially self-publishing authors, need to study their competition carefully. Read their books. Study your competition's book covers, the pricing, reviews, and their book marketing. These are the most powerful and essential steps you can take toward promoting your book begin long before the actual writing of the book. At least two years before the book is published, start building a network of supporters and reviewers.

Print Paperbacks and Hardcovers

Traditional publishers concentrate on print books, which still make up for about 60% of the book market (depending on if you look at book sales numbers or revenue per book.)

Audiobooks

The audiobook market is growing at a fast pace. Trade Publishers are not only investing in digital books (even so it took them a long time) but also in audiobooks. Read more about *the rise of audiobooks* – *https://www.forbes.com/sites/adamrowe1/2018/03/27/the-rising-popularity-of-audiobooks-highlights-the-industrys-backwards-payscale/#508766d94723* – which are up about 20% year over year across the publishing industry for the first eight months of 2017, according to the Association of American Publishers' data reports from 1,200 publishers. In the same time period, print books rose just 1.5%.

Paperback or Hardcover?

E-book authors might be happy with their sales on Amazon, Apple, Kobo or Barnes & Noble. You might have even turned it into an audiobook. But the questions about a "real" book, paperback or hardcover, from conservative friends or elderly family members are nagging. Besides, wouldn't it be nice to walk into a Chapters, Baker & Taylor, or one of those rare independent bookshops and see your book on the shelf?

You will not earn a fortune, maybe not even a living, but for a couple of months, it is nice pocket change. Yes, it will only last for a couple of months because barely any book will stay in the bookstore longer than this – unless it really is a bestseller and gets reprinted.

If you go the indie route and choose, for example, the print on demand (POD) services and worldwide distribution through LightningSource (provided you have at least ten books to be considered a small publisher), or *Amazon Direct Publishing* – *https://kdp.amazon.com/en_US/help/topic/G201857950* for fewer books, your book is printed on demand and will never get discarded. Another benefit is that there is a no-return policy in POD worldwide distribution – which has it's benefits but also drawbacks..

Book Sales at Many Outlets

Imagine if you could buy all the Penguin books only from a single book chain…Publishers distribute their books to as many outlets as possible: brick-and-mortar stores, independent booksellers, mass markets, hotels, airport news stores, online booksellers, even Affiliate programs.

Sell your books, e-books, and audiobooks not only through Amazon but also on Barnes & Noble, Apple and Kobo websites and all the other online retailers, mentioned in a former chapter. This will ensure that you have your "eggs in more than one basket". Also, don't forget the potentially huge market for hardcover books: selling them to libraries all over the country!

There are more online retailers for e-books and books than just Apple, Amazon, Kobo and Barnes & Noble! And sign up with a book distributor/fulfillment company for your print version of the book. Distributors require often just three books to be listed as a publishing business.

Suggested Books for Future Publishers:

Aaron Shepard has written two books about the topic of book distribution. They are called *POD for Profit* and *Aiming at Amazon*. Both of them contain detailed information for small publishers. Another great source is the late Dan Poynter's self-publishing manual, a classic publishing guidebook called *Content Writing for Magazines and Newspapers*.

Do What You Love Most: Writing

Marketing, promoting, and spending lots of time on social media are not activities authors cherish, but what about promoting books through your own writing? You can do what you love most and get paid at the same time. You know how to write a novel, but you also need to learn how to write shorter pieces and how to write for the web, where readers have shorter attention spans. All these skills can be acquired at classes on and offline, at workshops through writers' associations and beta-reading groups, at book fair programs, at writers' conferences, and certainly at college classes.

- Writing more books
- Writing short stories
- Writing prequels
- Writing sequels
- Writing blog articles
- Writing guest blogs
- Writing for literary contests
- Commercial Writing Examples:
- Writing for magazines
- Writing newspaper articles
- Writing website copy
- Writing resumes and cover letters
- Writing sales copy

Leverage your writing and your research:

These opportunities don't require you to create completely new stories or articles. In many cases, you can leverage your books and blogs and divide, rewrite, shorten, or add new content to chapters to "repurpose" your inventory. Another strategy is to use the content of your manuscript research and create new stories or articles.

For example, you could repurpose the research and content from a novel taking place in medieval Great Britain or a travelogue about a trip to Europe by writing an article about horse stables for equestrian magazines, one about the fantastic gardens in Great Britain for garden magazines, one about how to travel on a budget to European cities for a frugal living magazine, one about U.K. biking paths for a bike magazine, a feature about pumpkin seed pressing mills in Austria for gourmet magazines, one about a historic flax or wool mill in France for a sewing or craft magazine, a photo feature from a boutique hotel for a fine interior decorating magazine, one about dressing for city trips without looking like a tourist for fashion or lifestyle magazines… The possibilities are endless…

Writing for Magazines and Newspapers

World-famous bestselling writers from big publishing houses, such as Ernest Hemingway, Margaret Atwood, Tom Chiarella, Gloria Steinem, and Stephen King occasionally wrote (and still write) short stories and magazine articles before blogs became fashionable. Your book was launched months ago, or even last year. NOW readers need to see something NEW from you. It doesn't need to be a whole new book. The three main assets you have already are: your writing skills; the content you have already penned, and the research you have done for your book(s). Your research can be used to write at least twenty to thirty articles or blog posts. If you regularly post them on Google+, it will boost your Search Engine Ranking on Google tremendously.

Additional benefits of writing new content include the following:

- It is a subtle way to promote your book
- You will receive valuable backlinks to your website or blog

- You will have lots of opportunities to post on Twitter, Google+ and Pinterest
- You can include links to your articles in an e-mail newsletter (that you hopefully send out regularly to your readers)

Rewrite your articles and short stories a bit. Add more material and offer them to magazines, newspapers, and more, starting with these: airline inflight magazines (which pay the most), *Huffington Post* and *Salon.com*. Even *The Atlantic* might be interested in publishing your article if it is a longer article with exceptional content.

> IMPORTANT: Focus more on discoverability rather than selling. Your work is important, so help readers to find it. You can also post on your blog, or contribute guest blogs to other sites that are focused on the same topics as your book. Artists in other disciplines, such as musicians or ballet dancers, train six to ten hours a day. Become a prolific writer by doing the same. It pays; not only in financial terms.

A Great Example of How to Promote Your Book for Free in Magazines:

Author Steven Raichlen wrote an article for Huffington Post Foodie Paradise: *10 Great Places to Eat in Martha's Vineyard*. Steven Raichlen had his characters visit the same places that he usually patronizes with his wife in a salute to some of his favorite local eateries on Martha's Vineyard, including the following: restaurants, coffee shops, lobster shacks, and ice cream parlors. He writes in this article: "I hope you'll discover them by reading *Island Apart*. As my present to you and just in time for July 4th, here are 10 great places to eat in Martha's Vineyard, who knows, maybe you'll maybe run into Claire and the Hermit of Chappaquiddick …" He even adds a link to his book on Amazon, explaining that it is now available in paperback. Read the whole story about his free, brilliant book marketing *here – http://savvybookwriters.wordpress.com/2013/07/07/free-brilliant-book-marketing-to-a-million-audience/*.

Content is King!

Content is used to draw in your ideal readers/reviewers. It will link to your book sales page or your website, and it helps to build a platform. Last but not least: it gives you a lot of material to post and tweet. The result is that you will increase your exposure, show your writing skills, grow a loyal following, and attract reviewers. If I could sum it all up in one sentence: you will achieve success through writing. In many cases, you will even get paid for it. Because writing is what authors like to do, it's the perfect way of marketing for them! Even if they are "shy" writers.

Sampling is the Best Way to Hook a Reader

Retail businesses know the importance of sampling. Sample giveaways in grocery stores work! Then, there are the many samples arriving in the weekly flyers. Personal products, such as shampoo or body lotions, get promoted through hotels to their guests. Now, readers can download samples of any book published electronically. If they like the book, they will most likely buy it right away.

Bestseller Tips – From Trade Publishers

Press Kits on Your Website

Bestseller authors at traditional publishers have the support of the publisher's in-house (or outsourced) publicity department. How much publicity support the publisher gives depends on many factors. However, there are basic elements that a publicity department will likely provide: Book Press Materials. Near the publication date, the book's publicist will e-mail the electronic version of the press kits to a large number of applicable editors and producers to garner interest in the book. Book Media Follow-Up is the next step.

The book publicist will then follow these steps: follow up with any media outlet that responds to the mailings or e-mailings; mail additional copies of the finished book. And make additional calls or e-mails to other outlets (to remind them the book is in their in-box).

This is just a small selection of the many book marketing activities that authors can copy from major professional publishers. Find more suggestions and links in this *blog article* – *http://savvybookwriters.wordpress.com/2014/08/17/17-bestseller-tips-from-trade-publishers*.

Conclusion

Don't get overwhelmed by all the book marketing possibilities listed here. You don't have to do it all in a week, a month, or even a year. They are single steps you can take, one by one, to build your author platform and brand. These steps are long-term time investments. They won't initiate an immediate spike in book sales; rather, they will improve the number of your readers and the exposure of your books.

Self-publishing authors with only one book might be tempted to heavily promote their single title and postpone writing their next book. Even if 20,000 people bought your first book, and you take one or two years to finish the next title, readers will move onto other writers and forget you.

It's better to spend the main part of your day writing the next book, blogs, short stories or magazine articles. The best thing you can do to promote your writing is to write more! Remember, it takes at least FIVE successful books to make a living from writing. The good news is that all of your writing is an asset that will keep making you money for decades to come!

CHECKLIST FOR YOUR BOOK MARKETING

Before your manuscript is finished:

- Have a professional! photographer take a portrait to use for your avatar.

- Get to know and introduce yourself to potential readers by signing up on Google+ (good for SEO), Twitter, FB, Pinterest, and Flickr.

- Join several book communities: #1 Goodreads, #2 Wattpad, #3 KindleBoards, BookTalk, Scribd, etc.

- Visit forums in your field, especially if you write non-fiction.

- Start to write blog posts regularly (once or twice a week). – Create your own (not a free!) author website.

- Send your blog articles to newspapers, magazines, and blog directories.

- Write guest blogs for other bloggers in order to get your name out.

- Write your "elevator pitch" and practice your "elevator speech" for quick pitch.

- Start a spread sheet or list with e-mail addresses of potential readers.

- Create an e-mail signature and use it for every email you send out.

- Print business cards and book marks with an image of your book's cover

- Get an ISBN and register your copyright

- Register with Bowker.com to have your book listed worldwide for free.

Once your book is edited and has an appealing cover:

- Gather as many reviews as possible and write a compelling blurb.

- Invite several thousand! people as followers and friends on your social media sites.

- You Never Get a Second Chance to Make a Good First Impression.

- Get Pre-Orders For Your New Book.

- Produce a Print and Audiobook (free!)

- Place your book into the right category/genre and sub-genre.

- Create a second, separate BOOK PAGE/AUTHOR PAGE on Amazon, Goodreads, and Google+.

- Submit your book to the Library of Congress (USA only).

- Set up a media press kit on your website with a link to your book trailer.

- Plan and create an e-mail campaign to potential readers.
- Get customer orders for specially priced pre-launch sale.
- Invite more reviewers for your book.
- Submit photos of your book cover image to Pinterest, Flickr and Instagram.
- Create a slide show and/or video book trailer.
- Pitch book reviewers to various publications and book bloggers.
- Send review copies to book discussion clubs.
- Automate submissions to (and between) all your social networks.
- Write a blog post about the upcoming launch.
- Spruce up your website and blog for your book launch.
- Write a compelling press release.
- Ask your friends to list your book under "Listmania" on Amazon.
- Participate in "Carnival of the Indies" blog to promote your blog URL.
- Comment on other blogs and write lots of guest blogs.

- Consider participating in "Pay With a Tweet".
- Offer interviews at radio/TV stations and newspapers.
- Become a desirable guest expert on a talk or morning show.
- Befriend influential book bloggers for even more reviews and articles.
- Contact local libraries and offer a lecture.
- Contact local bookstores for book signings.
- Gather writing friends for cross-promotions and blog tours.
- Add press clippings and articles, already published, to your website.
- Get a new business card with an image of your book and sales link.
- Place the book's cover image and description on your Google+ stream daily.
- Announce your book launch or book signing on Google+ for FREE.
- Get even more friends, followers, and people in your circles on social media sites.

Other things you can do to increase your book's success:
- Sell your book to libraries.

- Get your book translated into other languages, or sell foreign rights.

- Split your (non-fiction) book up and sell single articles to magazines.

- Participate in writing contests and book awards.

- Become a guest speaker at writers' conferences or seminars.

If you found the information in this guide book useful, please leave a review on Amazon and Goodreads.

Thanks in advance!

About the author

Doris-Maria Heilmann has written a dozen books on publishing, marketing and aviation. She has more than 30 years experience in publishing, writing, (German and English) and in book marketing. She started her writing and teaching career in the field of commercial aviation and pilot training and published not only several books, but also her own successful flight and travel magazine "USA BY AIR", for a European audience of over 30,000 subscribers, and many more magazine buyers in three German-speaking countries.

Magazine and Book Publisher

She learned a lot in these years as a magazine publisher: editor-art-director-marketing-manager and later started also publishing books, mostly technical and non-fiction books in the world of aviation.

E-Publishing and Book Marketing

At Algonquin College in Ottawa, Canada, she studied e-publishing and marketing, including web and graphic design, professional photography, writing for the web, editing, investigative journalism, social media and e-marketing. Because e-publishing is always evolving, Doris continuously studies the e-book and traditional publishing market.

Seminars/Workshops/Public Speaking

The topics of her seminars and workshops (on- and offline) include: book design, establishing an author platform and brand, publishing, book marketing and promotional campaigns, social media, and print and e-book distribution.

She likes to travel long-distance with her dog "Bentley" and is an avid photographer. Her travel experiences in Canada and the USA can be found at her popular blogs

http://a-happy-traveler.blogspot.ca or on

http://marvelous-canada.blogspot.ca/

<><><><><>

Note to Readers

The information provided in this book is intended to provide helpful information on book marketing and publishing. We are not offering it as legal, accounting, or other professional services advice. While we have used our best efforts in preparing this book, we make no representations or warranties. In addition we assume no liabilities with respect to the accuracy or completeness of the contents.

Due to the speed at which changes occur in e-book technology, and how the self-publishing industry develops, no book about these topics can stay 100% up to date. Therefore we highly recommend that readers visit our blog and to sign up for the latest writing and publishing tips.

Find more Information about Successful Publishing on these Websites:

http://111Publishing.com/Seminars

http://Content-on-Demand.blogspot.ca

https://savvybookwriters.wordpress.com/

Let's Meet Here Too:

http://bit.ly/19PrQAz   Google+

http://bit.ly/VmtVAS   111Publishing @ Google+

http://bit.ly/13NFyBT   ebookPR @ Google+

http://www.goodreads.com/111publishing

http://www.international-ebooks.com

http://www.e-book-pr.com/

http://www.111Publishing.com/

https://www.linkedin.com/in/doris-maria-heilmann-65345595/

http://www.twitter.com/111publishing

http://www.twitter.com/ebookPR

http://www.twitter.com/ebooksIntl

http://pinterest.com/111publishing/

http://about.me/ebookPR

http://on.fb.me/TvqDaK

Find all my books here:

https://www.books2read.com/ap/n4EYY8/Doris-Maria-Heilmann

www.ingramcontent.com/pod-product-compliance
Lightning Source LLC
LaVergne TN
LVHW041335080426
835512LV00006B/471